A BETTER COUNTRY

ENDORSEMENTS

At a time when over 100 million people in the world—each of them created in the image of God—have been forcibly displaced from their homes by violence, persecution, wars, and turmoil, the church dares not turn a blind eye. Christ made it abundantly clear that our God cares deeply about the most vulnerable, and if we claim to be His followers, we must also. Individual believers, small groups, and local churches will be grateful that Cindy Wu's *A Better Country* provides biblical clarity and unique insights into the refugee experience and the US refugee resettlement infrastructure, and shows how God can use us to welcome, engage, serve, and partner with those He brings near. The spiritual practice sections of each chapter make us aware of how God can use our experiences with those who have lost everything to increase our dependence on Him, mature us spiritually, and grow our capacity to enjoy Him now and for eternity.

PAT HATCH
Refugee and Immigrant Ministry Director, PCA Mission to North America

More than a mere academic exercise, Cindy's passionate advocacy on behalf of refugees is an expression of her faith in Christ. Through her writing, teaching, training, advocacy, and personal involvement, Cindy embodies the spiritual practice of hospitality to the stranger rooted throughout Scripture, and she longs to see the body of Christ do the same. To that end, Cindy has written an exceptional tool for ministry leaders, small groups, non-profits, individuals, families, and communities to prepare them to come alongside refugees and other forcibly displaced persons with the love of God. We have had the privilege of working side-by-side with Cindy for years and have witnessed her living out these biblical truths. The principles in this book serve as a powerful and practical framework for those seeking to live out God's invitation to welcome the foreigner in our midst.

MICHAEL, MDIV, & JULIE MEISSNER
Co-founders, Abba's House of Texas

A Better Country is a thoughtful and clear introduction to the refugee crisis and the church's response. Cindy Wu untangles the complexity of refugee resettlement in the US and demystifies the first steps of building relationships with our neighbors who have experienced forced displacement. Set within a historical and biblical context that maintains honesty about the challenges, readers are left with a practical and hopeful path to live out the call to love our neighbors as ourselves.

SHANNA DOUGHTY, MA
Co-Facilitator, Refugee Highway Partnership North America (RHPNA)

Over several years I have watched Cindy Wu read, study, listen to, feel personally, and write about refugees and their situations in the United States. She has done so with deep compassion joined together with objective realism. This most timely workbook should be widely read and used in churches across our land.

DEAN BORGMAN, MA
Senior Professor of Youth Ministries and Social Ethics,
Gordon-Conwell Theological Seminary

Every Christian wishing to find the balance between security and compassion should work through *A Better Country*. Wu serves the church by presenting an excellent foundation for understanding refugee history, journey, and advocacy. This timely workbook presents facts to alleviate unnecessary fears in these important days.

DAVID DANIELS, DMin
Lead Pastor, Central Bible Church

Ms. Wu lives in Houston, America's most ethnically diverse city and practices the kind of hospitality she espouses. Out of her own experience and interest, she offers a workbook to help the reader learn about refugees and embrace the challenge of offering them hospitality. I envision a Sunday School class or home group using this valuable resource in a group study. Ms. Wu artfully combines facts, refugee stories, and words of challenge, for those who wish to serve others. She refers to Mariane from Rwanda in the Introduction and then quotes her in the book's Conclusion: "People have many freedoms here (USA) and hard work pays off. Close the door behind you and open another one. You don't have to live in between doors." That is the challenge Cindy Wu extends to her readers. Be a door-opener for the world's refugee peoples wherever you find them.

RICHARD L. HANEY, PhD
Executive Director, Frontier Fellowship

A Better Country is a book for such a time as this. More than 100 million people in the world have been forced to flee their homes and are seeking a better life. Cindy Wu provides a solid biblical, moral, and historical basis for welcoming refugees into our country and into our communities. *A Better Country* is a very practical guide for both churches and individuals, filled with resources and suggestions for how Christians can live out the biblical call to welcome the stranger.

DAVID HUSBY, MDiv
Retired Director, Covenant World Relief

At a time when the arrival of refugees is mired in misinformation and fear, Cindy Wu has created a fantastic, timely resource in *A Better Country*. With insightful analysis, biblical wisdom, and clear applications, this is a superb resource for Christians searching for a deeper understanding of refugees.

MATTHEW SOERENS, MS
US Director of Church Mobilization and Advocacy, World Relief

Cindy Wu's new book is a remarkable fusion of facts, personal experience, and biblical reflection on how Christians should treat migrants and strangers. As the West increasingly closes its heart, mind, and homelands to the rest of the world, this is a timely prophetic call to the church to follow Jesus's example and welcome the stranger. As a bonus, Wu's approach is highly practical, providing a much-needed tool for churches and small groups to study and to act.

TODD M. JOHNSON, PhD
Co-Director, Center for the Study of Global Christianity,
Gordon-Conwell Theological Seminary

Second Edition

A BETTER COUNTRY

Embracing the Refugees in Our Midst

Cindy M. Wu

WILLIAM CAREY PUBLISHING

Available at missionbooks.org

Published by William Carey Publishing
10 W Dry Creek Cir, Littleton, CO 90120 | www.missionbooks.org

Interior Designer: Mike Riester
Cover Designers: Josiah Wu and Mike Riester
Cover Illustrator: Josiah Wu, "The Hospitality of Abraham's Children"

William Carey Publishing is a ministry of
Frontier Ventures
Pasadena, CA | www.frontierventures.org

ISBNs: 978-1-64508-452-5 (paperback)
        978-1-64508-454-9 (epub)

Printed worldwide
26 25 24 23 22   2 3 4 5 6   IN

Library of Congress Control Number: 2022946775

CONTENTS

PREFACE

In 2009 I took a seminary course that would change the direction of my ministry calling. I was a student at Gordon-Conwell Theological Seminary in South Hamilton, Massachusetts, just beginning my degree. The course, titled "Biblical Global Justice," was taught by Dean Borgman, a spry, white-haired Episcopal priest with a passion for justice and for youth.

Professor Borgman's class was eye-opening and uncomfortable, in a sanctifying way. I had always cared about social issues but had never explored the theological foundations for justice. By this time I had already lived in several countries around the world—and among the poor in one of them—yet I was still so sheltered from some of the greatest suffering and injustices on earth. And I was limited not just in my experiences, but also in any deeper reflection on the subject. Professor Borgman's class challenged me to think about justice on a larger scale.

The following semester, I took a class, "Christianity in Asia, Africa, and Latin America," at Boston University with church historian Dr. Dana Robert. One of our required readings for the course was *Blood Brothers*, the memoir of Elias Chacour, a Palestinian Christian.[1] Chacour grew up in Galilee in peaceful co-existence with Jewish neighbors. In 1947, the United Nations partition of Mandatory Palestine turned Palestinian land over to Zionists, leading to civil war and resulting in death or displacement for over one million Palestinians. Chacour's village was obliterated, and his family fled. Chacour went on to study in Europe, and later in life, as the Israeli-Palestinian conflict raged on in his homeland, he found his high calling—to be a peacemaker between these two groups of "blood brothers."

I confess that before reading *Blood Brothers*, I had never wondered whether there were Christians in Palestine. I had never given thought to the experience of Palestinians who had been forced into exile. I had only pictured Palestinians as armed, turbaned PLO (Palestinian Liberation Organization) terrorists, based off what I had seen on the news. Humbled, I was confronted with my prejudice and one-sided thinking.

During seminary, God grew in me a concern for social justice in both local and global contexts. At the time, my husband and I felt called to ministry in the States, so the question for me, then, was how to blend my passion for global missions and social justice while staying in our home country. One day while sitting at my desk at the seminary library, God gave me clarity: refugees. My parents' immigrant background had already given me a heart for newcomers in America, and my combined interests in the nations and social justice could converge in welcoming and advocating for refugees. But first I had to learn more.

---

1 Chacour, with Hazard, *Blood Brothers*.

I started volunteering with a ministry to refugees in the Boston area. I also asked Professor Borgman to supervise a self-designed independent study on the global refugee crisis, and he graciously agreed. That study eventually became the basis of my graduation project. I then asked Dr. Todd Johnson, Director of the Center for the Study of Global Christianity, to advise my project, which, many edits later, is this workbook you are holding in your hands.

After graduation, my family returned to our hometown of Houston, Texas, and my husband and I, along with our three kids, began welcoming refugees, in one of America's top resettlement cities. One of the highlights of my friendship with refugees is my Orthodox Christian Iraqi friend, Abeer. Abeer frequently calls me her "sister." She and I have so little in common on the surface, yet we have been able to give and receive love to one another through simple acts of hospitality and assistance. I help her navigate the challenges of re-establishing life in a new city; she inspires me by her love and sacrifice for her family. She has also introduced me to some pretty tasty food! Over the years, I have continuously engaged myself in writing, teaching, and mobilizing Christians to welcome refugees, a ministry that has become a passion of mine.

The first edition of this workbook was published in 2017. In the following years, the world experienced change and conflict on an unprecedented scale, including a global pandemic that ground resettlement to a halt. The number of forcibly displaced persons skyrocketed in a short amount of time, raising existential questions about how to address the refugee crisis. As a mobilizer, I witnessed more people in my city volunteering to welcome refugees than ever before. That stimulated me to consider a second edition of *A Better Country*, one that was less bound to a specific time, more interactive, and stimulated deeper spiritual reflection. I hope this second edition will serve you and your Christian community well.

My faith compels me to welcome refugees ... will you join me?

INTRODUCTION

MARIANE'S STORY

The night Mariane Uwimana left her home in Rwanda in 1994, she didn't know where she was going.[1] She was eight months pregnant with her second child and afraid for her life. A civil war between the two majority ethnic groups in Rwanda—the Hutus and the Tutsis—resulted in one of the worst genocides in modern history. Neighbor slaughtered neighbor, friend betrayed friend. The country was awash in a bloodbath, and masses of people were fleeing the country, many on foot. With only the clothes on their backs, Mariane and her husband walked from their home, past piles of massacred bodies lining the roads, toward uncertainty.

They made their way to a refugee camp in Zaire (now the Democratic Republic of the Congo). Poverty and illness permeated the place; they encountered suffering every direction they turned. The Uwimanas sought relief. From the refugee camp they moved to Burkina Faso, where Mariane gave birth to their second son only two weeks after arrival. Life there was tough, but bearable. After a few months, both Mariane and her husband found jobs.

Although grateful to have preserved her life, in the struggle to survive Mariane felt like she had "lost herself." She had already lost all her earthly possessions, and now she was losing her identity. She became a shadow of who she was. Educated, capable, and strong, Mariane was now at the mercy of others. The Uwimanas appealed to the United Nations for refugee resettlement, hoping for a better outlook. After three years in Burkina Faso, they were finally approved for resettlement in the United States.

For decades the United States has resettled refugees. Refugees live in every state in the US, from major metroplexes to small towns.[2] Some people welcome this, but some are fearful or wary. Americans have long been conflicted over how to view refugees, how to vet them, how to integrate them into society … whether they belong here at all. And American Christians find themselves politically and ethically divided on this controversial and often volatile subject.

The Bible commands charity and hospitality to strangers and sojourners (see Lev 19:9–10 and 33–34, for example). Hence people who follow Jesus and take his Word seriously have a special mandate to address the needs of refugees. But the complexities of

---

1 Personal interview with author. Name changed for privacy.

2 Wyoming is the only state with no resettlement infrastructure, but refugees are welcome to move there.

the refugee system and concerns over national security often overshadow the call to justice and mercy. In fact, some Christians are calling for our country to close its doors to immigrants and refugees.

Regardless of where one stands on immigration reform, American Christians must acknowledge they have a role to play in the solution to the refugee crisis, one of the gravest humanitarian issues of our day. We cannot and must not isolate ourselves from this global phenomenon. As the debate on immigration intensifies, how will Christians respond to this growing population from every tribe and tongue? How can we do a better job embracing newcomers? How can we do better at loving mercy and doing justice? How can we *be* a better country for refugees?

HOW TO USE THIS WORKBOOK

This study aims to help Christians—specifically, Christians in the United States—think theologically and practically about the global refugee crisis. The workbook is divided into six lessons plus a Personal Action Plan as your concluding application. You can do the lessons on your own or in a group setting, though the group setting will provide greater benefit as you hear other perspectives. The response boxes within the chapters are for personal processing as you read; at the end of every chapter will be a set of questions designed for groups, although they are appropriate for individual study as well. Feel free to share your answers to the personal reflection questions during your group study time.

For this edition, I have included a spiritual formation practice at the end of every chapter, as it is my hope that this study will transform your mind, heart, *and* soul. Your group can decide if they want to do the spiritual formation practices together or individually (some practices may be more conducive to doing individually). For those of you new to spiritual practices, please visit my website for an introduction: www.cindymwu.com/a-better-country-2022.

If you are doing this workbook in a group, designate one person to facilitate or lead and remember to follow principles of group discussion.

DO:
- Be slow to speak, quick to listen.
- Allow everyone to speak their mind.
- Be respectful when someone disagrees with your opinion.

DO NOT:
- Monopolize the conversation.
- Judge someone's faith if they come to conclusions different from yours.
- Make personal attacks if someone disagrees with you.

The aim of this study is to inspire you to action in response to the refugee crisis. My prayer is that you will develop a heart to welcome refugees with compassion and dignity in Jesus's name.

Chapter 1

GLOBAL PEOPLE, GLOBAL PROBLEMS

We are all living in one big town. –Mary Pipher

BEFORE WE BEGIN

In this chapter you will learn about the modern-day global refugee crisis. We will make distinctions between the different types of migrants and learn how global protection for refugees got started.

What are the first three words or images that pop into your mind when you hear the word "refugee"? Write your answers below.

What fears or unknowns come to mind when you think about refugees resettling in the US?

Look around your home. Chances are your clothes, food, furniture, and appliances come from all around the world. This might be something you take for granted. Goods that once took weeks to arrive by slow boat can now be ordered online and delivered to your home within days, if not hours. You can access television and radio programming in multiple languages from your living room sofa or car, 24/7.

Look around our country's major cities. You see crowds in all colors. You can drive down Main Street and find restaurants serving cuisine from distant lands. There is nothing remarkable about this anymore.

Globalization has linked the peoples of the globe to one another. On the one hand, living in a globalized world creates a sense of connectedness and closeness; globalization has the potential to enhance development and reduce inequality. On the other hand, a global economy can cause social, political, and economic upheaval; problems that face a faraway part of the world now have nearby impact.

> *Displace* to displace means to force someone to leave their home, typically because of war, persecution, or natural disaster.

Today we are facing a crisis with worldwide reverberations—the global refugee crisis—considered the worst mass displacement since World War II, surpassing what was then the largest in history.

Why are so many people displaced today? Several factors contribute:

- *Economic deprivation*: Migrants are forced by poverty and lack of development to seek better economic opportunity as a means of basic survival.
- *Repression*: Political instability and corruption, often in the form of totalitarian regimes, deny citizens their human rights.
- *Environment*: Environmental degradation or natural disasters destroy the land. Political dynamics often worsen the impact of natural disasters.
- *Violence*: War and civil unrest can force people to flee in fear of their physical safety.
- *Persecution*: Discrimination or ill-treatment based on a person's identity, religion, or affiliation often turns into a threat on someone's life.

In our connected world, a forced migration crisis that takes place in one part of the world will inevitably impact other parts of the world. A crisis of a global scale requires a global, concerted response. In 1950 a global refugee protection regime was created to provide that response.

How many forcibly displaced persons are there in the world today? Visit the United Nations High Commissioner for Refugees website, www.unhcr.org, and write the number here: _____

Write down the name of one country where conflict is causing people to flee, perhaps some place you've heard about in the news.

What factors are contributing to the migration?

REFUGEE AND ASYLUM REGIME IN THE TWENTIETH CENTURY

The first international effort for refugees began in 1921 under the League of Nations with the collaboration of international humanitarian organizations. In order to address the large-scale refugee populations produced by World War II, the Office of the United Nations High Commissioner for Refugees (UNHCR) was created.

UNHCR was established in 1950, initially as a temporary body to specifically and exclusively address the needs of forcibly displaced Europeans in the aftermath of World War II. Today UNHCR is a permanent body within the United Nations, and its scope extends globally. There are various players in the international refugee protection regime, but the primary organization is UNHCR.

In the 1970s the United States settled hundreds of thousands of Southeast Asian refugees through an ad hoc Refugee Task Force with temporary funding. The sheer volume of refugees prompted Congress to pass the Refugee Act of 1980, the first comprehensive plan for refugee resettlement, which standardized resettlement services and created the US Refugee Admissions Program.[1]

DEFINING "REFUGEES": THE 1951 REFUGEE CONVENTION

To begin our discussion on refugees, it is important to know what we mean by "refugee." A refugee is someone seeking *asylum*—protection or shelter from danger. The inherent right of every human being to find protection is at the heart of the international asylum and refugee protection regime. In 1951 the Refugee Convention, a multi-lateral treaty signed at a special United Nations conference in Geneva, Switzerland, put forth this international standard for defining refugee status and rights:[2]

> A *refugee* is someone who is unable or unwilling to return to his/her country of origin owing to a well-founded fear of being persecuted for reasons of race, religion, nationality, membership of a particular social group, or political opinion. A refugee is outside of his country of origin.

---

1 National Archives Foundation "Refugee Act of 1980."

2 The United Nations Convention and Protocol provides this full definition of refugee in Article 1.A.2: For purposes of the present Convention, the term "refugee" shall apply to a person who: (2) ... owing to well-founded fear of being persecuted for reasons of race, religion, nationality, membership in a particular social group or political opinion, is outside the country of his nationality and is unable, or owing to such a fear, is unwilling to avail himself of the protection of that country; or who, not having a nationality and being outside the country of his former habitual residence, is unable or, owing to such fear, is unwilling to return.

> *Resettlement*: the selection and transfer of refugees from a State in which they have sought protection to a third state which has agreed to them—as refugees—with permanent resident status.[3]

While the definition of terms like "fear" and "persecuted" were intentionally left vague to afford maximum protection to those who qualified, the scope of "refugee" was originally very narrow, applying only to Europeans displaced by WWII and to "events occurring before 1 January 1951." A 1967 Protocol removed the geographic and temporal limitation of the original 1951 Convention to make refugee protection more expansive.[4]

But refugees are only one type of forced migrant. Understanding the distinction between refugees and other types of migrants will help clarify the issues surrounding forced migration. Keep these definitions in mind whenever you listen to conversations or news reports about refugees. Generic application of the term can lead to misunderstanding about the population this workbook is addressing—refugees. A refugee in the United States is someone who has been classified and vetted by the UNHCR and US governmental agencies.

Debate revolves around the classification and evaluation of refugee status for those displaced by environmental factors. Some have conflated all causes for displacement and apply the term "refugee" generically to anyone who has been forced from their home. For instance, the category "environmental" or "climate" refugee has been introduced in more recent years as the plight of victims of environmental disasters has been brought to light. One source estimates that more people have been displaced from their homes due to environmental disaster than war and conflict.[5] Still, the technical UNHCR definition for refugee applies only to those fleeing religious, political, and/or ethnic persecution. Currently there is no protocol for dealing with "environmental refugees," even though their predicament is often tied with political factors. In 2016 the United States gave a first-ever grant to move a community impacted by climate change.[6]

> We must find a way to manage this crisis in a more humane, equitable, and organized manner. It is only possible if the international community is united and in agreement on how to move forward.
>
> —FILIPPO GRANDI,
> United Nations High Commissioner on Refugees,
> 2016-current.

---

3 UNHCR Resettlement Handbook 2011, 3.

4 Refugee advocates disagree on what constitutes a "refugee." Some refugee advocates suggest the Refugee Convention needs to be broadened further still to include victims of environmental devastation, economic deprivation, or violence. This would result in an even greater number of those classified as refugees.

5 Internal Displacement Monitoring Centre.

6 Davenport and Robertson, "Resettling the First 'Climate Refugees.'" The majority of those impacted by the climate crisis and move belong to the Biloxi-Chitimacha-Choctaw tribe of Louisiana.

Asylum seekers have already entered the land where they seek protection and are appealing for authorization to remain there. Asylum seekers have to be able to present a legitimate case for protection based on persecution, or they risk deportation. The right to seek asylum is enshrined in international law.

Asylees have legally received asylum. Asylees are eligible for Refugee Cash Assistance (RCA) and other benefits, like job training.

Internally displaced persons (IDP) have been forcibly removed from home but remain within the boundaries of their country of origin. IDPs constitute the largest category of forced migrants, but there is no international legal instrument to protect them.[7]

How many Internally Displaced Persons (IDP) are in the world today? Visit the Internal Displacement Monitoring Centre (IDMC), www.internal-displacement.org, and write the number here: _____

On the IDMC website, locate the Global Report on Internal Displacement. Which countries have the most internal displacements? What other data in the report do you find enlightening?

Why is it helpful to know the distinction between the different types of forced migrants? In your opinion, which type of forced migrant makes the most compelling case for protection?

---

7 Other persons of concern to the UNHCR are stateless persons—those who are not considered citizens of any political state under national laws, have no legal status, and are therefore deprived of many rights and benefits—and returned refugees (returnees) or returned IDPs—those who have returned voluntarily to their country of origin or area of habitual residence. Going home does not mean the need for protection has ended.

ASSESSING THE PROBLEM

What were the first words or images of refugees that you wrote down at the beginning of this chapter? Perhaps images of glassy-eyed masses stumbling out of boats. Perhaps bedraggled mobs limping across a dusty desert. Perhaps terrorists came to mind.

One barrier to welcoming refugees is our perception of them. Our mental images are heavily influenced by the media, and while there are plenty of stories of the positive contributions of refugees, much that is out there is negative.

What negative stereotypes have you seen (or held) about refugees? Try to come up with at least four:

What or who most influences your perception of refugees?

It is hard to welcome someone if we have a negative perception of them. Initially, worldwide population movements were viewed as a way to meet labor demands of growing economies. Today, however, a sudden influx of migrants to neighboring states is often viewed as a threat to national security, the economy, and cultural identity.

Refugees and national security were a major talking point in the 2016 presidential election. Republican party nominee Donald Trump proposed closing America's doors to outsiders, part of his platform to "Make America Great Again." Besides threatening to halt refugee admissions, especially from Syria, Trump proposed a temporary block of all Muslim immigration, mass deportation of undocumented immigrants, and a wall to keep out asylum seekers. In an April 2016 speech in Rhode Island, he mentioned that the state was resettling refugees, eliciting a chorus of boos. He then warned his audience, saying:

> We don't know where they're from … they have no documentation. We all have hearts, and we can build safe zones in Syria, and we'll get the Gulf States to put up the money … I'll get that done … We can't let this happen … Lock your doors … We don't know anything about 'em! … We have our incompetent government people letting 'em in by the thousands, and who knows, who knows, maybe it's ISIS.[8]

8 Engel, "Trump on Syrian Refugees."

Meanwhile, several Democrats in the House of Representatives defied President Barack Obama's decision to raise the resettlement ceiling by voting for a bill that would halt Syrian refugee resettlement by adding an additional layer of screening to their vetting process. (The bill was later blocked by the Senate.) At least two Democratic governors opposed Syrian refugee resettlement in their states. The growing anti-immigrant sentiment over the past decade is nothing new; our country has experienced waves of resistance to immigration, sometimes resulting in harsh exclusion laws.[9]

No matter your political persuasion, the reality is that refugees have come to America, and until the wars stop, refugees will continue to flow (not flood) into our country. In the past, refugee flows were thought to be temporary; today there are several protracted (long-lasting) situations all over the world, with refugees living in camps for 5, 10, even 25+ years! The global community is facing a global quandary: as the number of forcibly displaced people increases, will the resources to care for them be available? Who is responsible for refugees? What is the best way to help them? What has been our nation's role, if any, in *contributing* to displacement? We need to think seriously about our stance toward refugees.

Followers of Jesus must consider not only political solutions but, more importantly, what the Bible teaches about caring for those who suffer. We need a theological perspective on the refugee crisis. Let's learn a little more about the history and current dynamics of the modern-day refugee crisis, and then we'll look at what the Bible has to say about welcoming refugees.

> All human beings are born free and equal in dignity and rights. Everyone has the right to recognition everywhere as a person before the law. We recall that our obligations under international law prohibit discrimination of any kind on the basis of race, colour, sex, language, religion, political or other opinion, national or social origin, property, birth or other status. Yet in many parts of the world we are witnessing, with great concern, increasingly xenophobic and racist responses to refugees and migrants.
>
> –New York Declaration I.13, U.N. Summit for Refugees and Migrants (2016)

REFLECTION QUESTIONS

1. Write down ways in which globalization has impacted your daily life, both positively and negatively.

---

9 I recommend Yang, *One Mighty and Irresistible Tide*, for a recent overview.

2. How does the United Nations define "refugee"? What distinguishes a refugee from other types of forced migrants?

3. If refugees are resettled in your city, what concerns do you have about their presence? If there are none, how open are you to welcoming refugees?

4. Write down one Scripture that speaks to how God might view refugees. If needed, use your concordance to look up key words: "stranger," "sojourner," "foreigner."

5. Pause for a moment and ask God to prepare your mind and heart to be challenged by this study. What does he want you to learn, and how does he want you to respond? Ask him to remove any prejudices you may harbor.

Spiritual Practice: *Visio Divina*

Visio divina in Latin means "divine seeing." Before we move forward with our study, I invite you to ask God to help you see refugees through his eyes. Do a basic internet search and find a photo of refugees that draws you in. You may also use the cover art of this workbook. Scan the entire photo. Are your eyes being draw to certain parts? Allow your eyes to focus on one area of the photo and pause; take three deep breaths.

Now allow your eyes to take in the entire photo again.

- What emotions arise?

- What questions are getting stirred?

- What prayers are rising as you gaze at the photo?
  In the space below, write out a prayer to God.

Chapter 2

THE RUBBLED PLACES

The ruins in their hearts
Rehearse the rubbled places;
Our disordered times are
Recited by their faces.
The evils of our era
Are scrawled upon their features.
Who can scrub our History
From these ravaged creatures?
–Louis Ginsberg (1960)

BEFORE WE BEGIN

Chapter 2 shares refugee stories and gives a picture of the scope of the global crisis. We'll also look back at historical mass migration movements.

Go to your computer and type two words into your browser: "refugee" and the name of your city. What do you find? Are there refugee agencies in your city? Do you find any articles about refugees in your city? If your city has refugees, what parts of the city do they live in? How large is the refugee community in your city? What countries do they come from? Do some research to answer these questions.

Sara, an engineering professor, grew up in conflict-ridden Iraq with seven siblings, all high academic achievers. Violence surged during the Iraq War of the 2000s, and when Sara started receiving death threats, she knew it was time to leave. She left Iraq for Egypt, returning home three months later to officially resign her university post. The day she decided to resign, her brother, also a professor, went missing. Tragically, he was later found dead.[1]

Santino is one of tens of thousands of "Lost Boys" who were orphaned during Sudan's civil war of the 1980s. Some of the Lost Boys walked one thousand miles on foot seeking refuge in neighboring Ethiopia and Kenya, many dying on the treacherous trek across the desert. Some of them were abducted or conscripted by both rebel and government armies and trained as child soldiers. In total, 20,000 Lost Boys were displaced during the war.[2]

Victoria's mom was pregnant with her when she fled the civil war in Bosnia to the UK. Victoria's dad was held in a Serbian prison camp but later released. Between 1992 and 1995, over 200,000 Bosnians died in the horrific ethnic cleansing campaign.[3]

Omidullah's family fled Afghanistan on a Special Immigrant Visa designed to resettle Iraqis and Afghans who served the US military. He brought four of his children to Houston, leaving his eldest daughter, who was married, behind with her husband and baby. In August 2021, the Taliban overtook Kabul, resulting in a sudden mass migration out of Afghanistan. Families were separated and documentation was lost in the scuffle to flee. In the end over 120,000 Afghans were evacuated, with about 70,000 of those coming to the US, most of whom had to be processed at military bases. Omidullah's brother-in-law and father-in-law were able to come to Houston after waiting eight months in the United Arab Emirates; the combined impact of COVID and immigration processing delays have delayed resettlement for his daughter's family and thousands of other Afghans.[4]

As these stories reveal, refugees come in all colors, ages, languages, and from all walks of life. And they each share a story of individual and collective suffering from circumstances they did not expect or deserve. These stories remind us that behind each individual human face is a personal story.

It would be a mistake to view refugees as a monolithic horde of faceless people. The word "refugee" is not a label we should use to completely define someone. Before fleeing, many refugees were doctors, engineers, artists, community activists, athletes. Refugees have dreams they still want to pursue, and they have the right to self-determination as much as any other person. Followers of Jesus believe that, ultimately, refugees are people made in the image of God.

---

1 Personal interview with author. Name changed for privacy.

2 Mylan and Shenk, "Lost Boys of Sudan."

3 Naidoo, *Making It Home*, 19.

4 "Omidullah" is a personal friend of the author. For information on the Afghanistan evacuation, visit Department of Homeland Security Operation Allies Welcome: www.dhs.gov/allieswelcome.

Refugees are more than a statistic, but the numbers help us get a sense of the scope of the issue. This chapter provides some facts on historical and current refugee movements. As you read, remember that behind each statistic is a human being made in the image of God, a human being whose story is worth telling.

Referring back to your answer in Chapter 1, how many forcibly displaced persons are there worldwide? Use the UNHCR website as your source: www.unhcr.org.

How many of these are classified as refugees?

What are the top 3 refugee-producing situations at this time?

As of this writing, there are over 100 million forcibly displaced persons around the world, the highest number in recorded history.[5] This grim milestone in displaced persons reflects a sudden surge from the previous year due to war and invasions, revealing how quickly the overall picture of displacement can change.

- One quarter are refugees, defined as people outside the borders of their country of origin.
- The majority of displaced persons are women and children.
- Millions of refugees have lived in protracted situations for decades.
- A majority of the world's refugees live in urban areas.

The UNHCR defines a protracted refugee situation as one in which 25,000 or more refugees from the same nationality have been in exile for five or more years in a given asylum country.

---

5 UNHCR, "More than 100 Million Are Forcibly Displaced."

HISTORICAL FORCED MIGRATION MOVEMENTS

The modern refugee movement originated in Europe, but over the decades since World War II, changes in global politics have created refugee movements all around the world. This table will familiarize you with some of the major historical refugee movements in the past century and help you see why an international protocol was inevitable and necessary.

Table 1. Historical Forced Migration Movements[6]

1920s	• Russian Revolution • Armenian genocide (first large-scale humanitarian effort in the US)
1930s	• Europeans flee totalitarian governments • Rise of Nazis
1940s	• WWII and Holocaust[7] • Arab-Israeli conflict and exodus of Palestinians • 1947 Partition of India • 1949 Communist takeover in China
1950s	• Cold War and proxy wars • Korean War • Hungarian Revolution • Decolonization movements and civil wars in Africa and Asia
1960s	• Cuban Communist dictatorship • Latin American dictatorships
1970s	• "Boat people" flee Communist uprisings in Indochina • "Killing fields" of Cambodia • Bangladesh war of independence • Soviet invasion of Afghanistan
1980s	• Iran-Iraq War (1980–1988) • Corruption and violence in Central America and the Caribbean • Guerilla warfare in Colombia • Fall of Berlin Wall

---

6 This is a snapshot, not a comprehensive list. One unique resource is De Pillis, "Visual Guide to 75 Years." See also US Citizenship and Immigration Service, "Immigration and Naturalization."

7 World War II produced over 40 million refugees, considered the largest forced migration event in modern history and the impetus for the international refugee response.

1990s	• Gulf War • Civil war in Mozambique • Breakup of Yugoslavia • Dissolution of USSR • Civil strife in Bangladesh, Tibet, Myanmar (Burma) • First and Second Congo Wars • Rwandan genocide
2000s	• Bombing of World Trade Center and subsequent intervention in Afghanistan • (Note: Many of the refugee flows in the 2000s are ongoing from the previous century.)
2010s	• South Sudanese civil war • Ethnic and religious conflict in Central African Republic • Arab Spring and Syrian uprising • "Refugee highway": flows from Middle East to Europe and North America
2020s	• Taliban takeover of Afghanistan • Russian invasion of Ukraine • Decade of political corruption and economic crisis in Venezuela

As we have seen, multiple factors cause the number of refugees and the countries of origin of refugees to change over time. Less than a decade ago the composition of the world's refugees was quite different. Circumstances can change suddenly and unexpectedly. As of this writing Syrians constitute a significant portion of refugees; Syrian themselves never would have predicted this ten, even five years ago. Last year, there was no Ukrainian refugee crisis; today, it is one of the most critical situations.

Of the above historical events, write down the conflicts you were not aware of.

Select one historical event and jot down some notes about the cause of refugee flow.

What's missing from this list? Is there a refugee-producing conflict you are aware of that is not included?

ASSESSING THE REFUGEE CRISIS AT HOME

After a refugee is approved by UNHCR for resettlement in the US, individual states, non-governmental organizations (NGOs), and nine resettlement agencies receive funding to provide resettlement services for refugees.[8] In addition, churches, non-profits, and individuals contribute to refugee resettlement. Together, these entities mobilize volunteers to support refugees as they integrate into their new lives.

As you continue to learn about the refugee crisis, hopefully one of the questions you're asking yourself is, "How am I to respond?" One of the goals of this workbook is to provide a theological framework as the foundation for welcoming refugees resettled in America. In the next lesson, we'll look at what the Bible has to say about "strangers." You'll discover that as followers of Jesus we have a lot more in common with refugees than we realize.

REFLECTION QUESTIONS

1. What new or unexpected information did you learn in this chapter?

2. Go back and slowly look over the table of historical forced migration movements. What emotions are you feeling as you read the list?

---

8 See Appendix A for a full list of resettlement agencies.

3. What are your thoughts on an international coordinated effort to resolve the global refugee crisis? Was the response appropriate? How well is it working?

4. If you are going through this workbook with a group, share the research you did on historical forced migration movements. If doing this on your own, choose one additional situation and do some research on that conflict.

5. When was a time in your life when God took something broken and made it whole again?

Spiritual Practice: Nature Walk

This chapter is entitled "The Rubbled Places." Rubbled places are broken down, destroyed. But God can make beauty from ashes (Isa 61:3), and he can redeem the broken (Deut 30).

If you are physically able, go outside for a 15-minute nature walk. Observe God's creation and see if you can spy any dead leaves or grass. Does anything look "destroyed?"—an ant bed, a branch?

Next, look and listen for signs of life: buds, sprouts, animals, the sun, a moving stream. Thank God for his redeeming love and pray that refugees around the world would feel hope today.

Chapter 3

YOU WERE ONCE STRANGERS

For we are strangers before you and sojourners, as all our fathers were.
Our days on the earth are like a shadow, and there is no abiding.
–1 Chronicles 29:15

BEFORE WE BEGIN

Is it a biblical mandate to welcome refugees? Chapter 3 will challenge you to think theologically about how God looks at the "stranger."

Give one biblical example of a refugee or sojourner. What were some of the challenges this person faced?

If you have ever traveled outside of your home country, what was it like being a "stranger" in a foreign land? Name both positive and negative experiences and impressions.

Jesus said the two Greatest Commandments are to love God with all your heart, soul, and mind, and to love your neighbor as yourself (Matt 22:36–40). As the Greatest Commandment, "Love God" is naturally the most oft-repeated commandment in the Hebrew Scriptures. "Welcome the stranger" is the second.[1] Does that come as a surprise to you?

---

1 Quoting Orlando Espin in Soerens and Yang, *Welcoming the Stranger*, 85.

Welcoming the stranger is a non-negotiable part of the Christian ethic. It's what Christians do; at least, it's what we're supposed to do. The Scriptures can help us reclaim that old religious vision of welcoming the stranger.[2]

We begin with the historical narrative of the Jewish people, whose story began with sojourning. You will recall that each of the great patriarchs spent part of his life as a stranger in a foreign land. God called Abram out of Ur of the Chaldeans to leave his country, relatives, and inheritance and go to Canaan (Gen 12). His long journey took him from Haran to Canaan, then to Egypt to escape a famine, then back toward Canaan, where he eventually settled and had Isaac (Gen 21). Isaac and his son Jacob lived as sojourners throughout Canaan for two generations until Jacob and his sons (the tribes of Israel) settled in Egypt, where they stayed for four hundred years on account of a great famine (Gen 47). In Egypt they grew into a great nation. God eventually delivered Israel from Egyptian oppression through Moses, who led them toward the Promise Land. Along the journey, the Israelites encountered non-Israelites, some of whom chose to live among them as strangers.

> Besides the commandment to love God, "welcome the stranger" is the second most oft-repeated command in the Hebrew Scriptures.

Write out Leviticus 19:33–34 in its entirety. Underline any words or phrases that stand out to you.

THE STRANGER WHO SOJOURNS AMONG YOU

The Hebrew word for "stranger" is *ger*. Different Bible translations may also render the word *ger* as "alien," "foreigner," "guest," or "sojourner." The most accurate way to understand *ger* is as a resident immigrant.[3] In the Israelite community, a *ger* was a person living away from one's home country, who dwelled among the Israelites.

---

2 This vision is shared by the three Abrahamic faiths. See the Qur'an 93:6–11 and Sacks, "Loving the Stranger."

3 Vine, *Vines's Complete Expository Dictionary*, 237. For those interested in doing a word study of *ger*, its Strong's number is 1616. *Ger* occurs 92 times in the Old Testament.

The term generally referred to non-Israelites sojourning with the Israelites but was also applied to the Israelites themselves when they sojourned in Egypt (Exod 2:22). The sojourner had abandoned home for political or economic reasons and sought refuge among another community, as did Abraham in Hebron (Gen 23), Moses in Midian (Exod 22), Elimelech and his family in Moab (Ruth 1), Ruth by following Naomi to Judah (Ruth 1), and the Israelites in Egypt (Exod 1).

Ger is applied to those who settled in the land and sought the benefits and blessings of the land as prescribed by the law of Moses. Sojourners traveling with the Israelites were expected to respect their laws and were entitled to their protection and provision. And just as sojourners were to share in Israel's blessings (Deut 26:11), they were also subject to the laws of the land:

> For the assembly, there shall be one statute for you and for the stranger who sojourns with you, a statute forever throughout your generations. You and the sojourner shall be alike before the LORD. One law and one rule shall be for you and for the stranger who sojourns with you. (Num 15:15–16)[4]

Sojourners could participate in Jewish rituals as long as they followed Israel's laws for purification, circumcision, worship, and sacrifice (Deut 16:11; Exod 12:48). The Fourth Commandment makes provisions for strangers to enjoy Sabbath rest along with the Israelites so they may be refreshed (Exod 20:8; cf. Deut 5:14; Exod 23:12; Lev 16:29).

Israel played host to these foreign guests and was expected to protect, serve, love, and show hospitality to them: "You shall treat the stranger who sojourns with you as the native among you, and you shall *love him as yourself*, for you were strangers in the land of Egypt: I am the LORD your God" (Lev 19:34, emphasis added). The Israelites were to provide for the stranger by dividing food, tithe, blessing, and land (Deut 26:12; Ezek 47:21–23). The stranger did not have to earn status to be treated with concern and respect—God commanded it (Lev 19:33–34).

In legal matters, the Israelites were not to show partiality or withhold justice (Deut 1:17; 24:14, 17; 27:19). The Bible very clearly mandates against mistreatment and oppression of strangers; in fact, some of Israel's blessings and judgment were contingent upon how they treated the stranger.[5] It was the Israelites' responsibility to make sure the poor and the stranger were provided for:

> You shall not pervert the justice due to the sojourner or to the fatherless …
> —Deuteronomy 24:17

---

4 Cf. Exod 12:49; Lev 24:22; Num 15:29

5 See Deut 24:19; 26:15; Jer 7:6; 22:3; Ezek 22:7, 29; Zech 7:10; Mal 3:5.

When you reap the harvest of your land, you shall not reap your field right up to its edge, neither shall you gather the gleanings after your harvest. And you shall not strip your vineyard bare, neither shall you gather the fallen grapes of your vineyard. You shall leave them for the poor and for the sojourner: I am the LORD your God. (Lev 19:9–10; cf. Lev 23:22)[6]

Strangers among the Israelites were to be treated with equality, like natives of the land. Therefore caring for refugees isn't just a compassion or pity issue—it's a justice issue. God in his righteous justice cares for all people, and so should we.

What is the basis for viewing caring for refugees as a justice issue?

Do you agree with this assessment; why or why not?

DO JUSTICE, LOVE REFUGEES

Laws were set in place to protect sojourners among the Israelites. God's heart for justice was revealed through those laws and in the pronouncements he made against false justice (Isa 58). It's not enough to love the Word, study theology, tithe, share your faith, and abide by the law. It's not enough to do many things well—like the Pharisees—and yet lack one thing: "Woe to you … you hypocrites! You have a tenth of your spices—mint, dill and cumin. But you have neglected the more important matters of the law—justice, mercy, and faithfulness" (Matt 23:23).

Jesus calls us beyond the letter of the law. Besides teaching the Greatest Commandment: "Love the Lord your God … Love your neighbor as yourself" (Matt 22:37–39), Jesus also taught: "Love your enemies and pray for those who persecute you" (Matt 5:44). In the Parable of the Good Samaritan (Luke 10:25–37), a victim of violence was cared for and provided for by a Samaritan, considered to be an outsider to Jewish society. Jesus praised the Samaritan for being a true neighbor to the fallen man. In the same way, we fulfill the Greatest Commandment by caring for and providing for those who have suffered much, especially those who are different from us.

During Jesus's earthly ministry he redefined social norms and overturned economic principles. He welcomed the outcast into his fellowship. He called people to give up their earthly treasures for a heavenly promise. He taught that

---

6 Other provisions for the stranger: Deut 14:29; 24:14–22.

the first would be last and the last would be first. He fed thousands with scraps of food. It is this kind of radical love and behavior that Jesus calls his followers into.

He has told you, O man, what is good; and what does the Lord require of you but to do justice, and to love kindness, and to walk humbly with your God?   —Micah 6:8

NO PROMISED LAND

From the first patriarch, Abraham, to Jesus and his disciples, and then to the church, God has revealed himself as a God whose heart loves all the nations (Ps 2:8; Isa 51; John 3:16). In Genesis 12:1–3 God calls Abraham:

> Now the LORD said to Abram, "Go from your country and your kindred and your father's house to the land that I will show you. And I will make of you a great nation, and I will bless you and make your name great, so that you will be a blessing. I will bless those who bless you, and him who dishonors you I will curse, and in you all the families of the earth shall be blessed."

God chose to bless Abraham by first turning him into a refugee. This was not a punishment but rather part of God's plan for the salvation of the nations (Acts 7:6). During his sojourn Abraham was compelled to seek the protection and favor of the Egyptians, Philistines, and Hittites. It appears to have been difficult at times for Abraham to see how God would fulfill his promise (Gen 16:2), but Abraham believed God and it was counted to him as righteousness (Rom 4:9).

In Genesis 12, when God called Abraham and his family out of his homeland, God made a promise to Abraham—that he would give him a land to possess and fill with his descendants, who would be as numerous as the stars in the sky. Abraham and his descendants spent most of their lives sojourning before they were able to enter the Promised Land. Today, the Middle East is still the land of sojourn for millions of people, not because of promise, but as a consequence of war, conflict, and persecution.

Shortly after Jesus's birth King Herod issued an order to kill all infant boys in his attempt to get rid of the newborn king (Matt 2:13–14). Jesus, Mary, and Joseph fled from Galilee and found refuge in Egypt as sojourners. And Jesus wasn't a sojourner just once. In fact, his entire ministry on earth was itinerant. Jesus was constantly on the move from those who would do him harm. Our Lord and Savior himself lived the experience of a refugee!

YOU WERE ONCE STRANGERS

As you can see, the sojourner metaphor is deeply embedded within the history and theology of the Jewish people. Being a stranger and sojourner is part of their identity, and so it gets transmitted down as heritage to us as followers of Jesus Christ:

- "You shall not oppress a sojourner. You know the heart of a sojourner, for you were sojourners in the land of Egypt" (Exod 23:9).
- "For you are strangers and sojourners with me" (Lev 25:23).
- "For I am a sojourner with you, a guest, like all my fathers" (Ps 39:12).
- "I am a sojourner on the earth" (Ps 119:19).
- "Beloved, I urge you as sojourners and exiles to abstain from the passions of the flesh, which wage war against your soul" (1 Pet 2:11).

The stranger motif is powerful because it describes our relationship to God before Christ, as well as our relationship to our heavenly home. Before Christ, Gentiles (the nations) "were separate from Christ, excluded from citizenship in Israel and foreigners to the covenants of the promise, without hope and without God in the world" (Eph 2:12). But then God adopted us into his family through Jesus Christ, and we are "no longer strangers and aliens" (Eph 2:19). Christ has torn down the separating wall and we are no longer strangers to God—instead, we are his children (Eph 1:5; 2:14).

The heart of God toward strangers back then and today is that of a loving and protective Father (Ps 146:9). Resist, then, the urge to allow the word "refugee" to become a label that creates a wall between you and the stranger. Christians today are called to have this heart towards strangers: "[God] executes justice for the fatherless and the widow, and loves the sojourner, giving him food and clothing. Love the sojourner, therefore, for you were sojourners in the land of Egypt" (Deut 10:18–19). Throughout Scripture the Lord reminds his people that they, too, had once been in the same needy position as the stranger.

Like refugees, all we who are in Christ are considered sojourners, aliens, and pilgrims on earth (1 Chr 29:15; 1 Pet 1:17). Like the giants of the faith listed in Hebrews 11, we acknowledge that we are strangers and exiles on the earth. Yet as strangers and exiles we are not aimless, nor are we hopeless. Rather, we desire a better country, a heavenly one (Heb 11:16). As sojourners we make no claim to this life or this land. We recognize that everything we have is by God's will and by his grace. And so we fix our eyes on heaven, where our true citizenship lies: "Our citizenship is in heaven, and from it we await a Savior, the Lord Jesus Christ" (Phil 3:20).

We can relate with refugees because we, too, have no permanent home in this life. This is what we have in common—we are all looking for a better country. And by that token we all depend on the grace of God.

REFLECTION QUESTIONS

1. Summarize the meaning and significance of the word *ger*. How does the biblical treatment of "strangers" impact the way you view refugees?

2. How does Jesus's own identification as a refugee and as a sojourner on earth impact the way you view refugees? How does it impact the way you view yourself?

3. Do you have personal contact with refugees? If so, how has knowing them impacted you?

4. Who are the "strangers" in your life? Who are people you encounter on a regular basis that perhaps you have been avoiding or have not extended a welcome to?

5. In what ways are you behaving too much like a citizen of the earth rather than a citizen of heaven in search of a better country? What rights, privileges, or material things are you holding on to that aren't yours to claim? Pray and ask God to reveal this to you. Respond with humility knowing that God looks upon us with compassion.

Spiritual Practice: *Lectio Divina*

Lectio divina in Latin means "divine reading." *Lectio divina* is a slow, reflective, and meditative reading of Scripture that allows you to absorb the Word of God. A typical lectio is guided by the Holy Spirit in steps or movements.

This chapter contains many Scripture references. Select one that was meaningful to you and circle it in the workbook. To begin your lectio, close your eyes and take three deep breaths, letting your body relax and your mind become fully present to the moment. Now, slowly, read out loud the verse or passage you selected. Pause and ponder on the meaning of the text and how it's touching you.

Next, read the text again, slowly, aloud or silently. What is your response? Pause and pray back to God whatever you are sensing. Finally, read the text a final time, slowly. Rest in whatever God is speaking to you or however he's leading you to respond.

Chapter 4

The Pilgrim's Problem

"If we knew the stories of refugees, they would break our hearts."
–Garrison Keillor

BEFORE WE BEGIN

Chapter 4 looks at adversities faced by refugees. As you read this chapter try to imagine yourself in the shoes of refugees who have found themselves in these dire predicaments.

In the last lesson, we identified with refugees out of our inherited sojourner heritage as the people of God. What are some common challenges faced by sojourners on the move?

Imagine leaving your homeland for a new country. What would you miss leaving behind the most?

On May 13, 1939, the *St. Louis* sailed from Germany to Cuba with 937 refugees on board. Almost all passengers were Jews fleeing the Third Reich. Most held landing certificates and transit visas issued by the Cuban government, unaware that a week prior the Cuban president had invalidated their legal documents. Denied entry by Cuba, the *St. Louis* headed toward Miami to seek refuge in the United States. The pleas to admission by an American Jewish refugee organization, the ship's captain, and the passengers were to no avail—the *St. Louis* was forced to sail back to Europe. The passengers were admitted to four Western European countries where they were interned in labor camps or were forced to go into hiding. Some were later able to emigrate to North America or Australia. Many were later deported and exterminated in Nazi concentration camps after the German invasion of Western Europe.[1]

Three-quarters of a century later, on April 19, 2015, a small vessel set sail from Libya, steering toward Italy. The boat, dangerously overloaded with migrants and refugees, capsized, leading to the deaths of an estimated 800 people in the waters of the Mediterranean Sea, the deadliest disaster there to date.[2] The following year, during three consecutive days, three more boats capsized, plunging 700 migrants to their watery graves.[3] Between 2013 and 2016 at least 10,000 migrants lost their lives trying to cross the sea.[4]

Many questions arise from the tragic stories of the *St. Louis* and the Mediterranean Sea crossings: Did the refugees have a "right" to seek refuge abroad? Do the countries where they are trying to land have a moral obligation to admit them? How does a state struggling internally with low employment and recession handle immigration requests? How does a state counter xenophobia, racism, and fear? These and other questions reveal there is no simple solution to the refugee crisis.

Did the passengers have a "right" to seek refuge abroad? Do destination countries have an obligation to receive migrants?

What emotions get stirred as you read about these tragedies?

NO EASY SOLUTIONS

A durable solution is one that will enable refugees to live in safety and rebuild their lives.
–United Nations High Commissioner for Refugees, "Solutions"

Ultimately the goal of UNHCR is to ensure refugees' access to protection and a *durable solution*. UNHCR seeks to employ one of three durable solutions:

---

1 For more on the *St. Louis*, search the United States Holocaust Memorial Museum website: http://www.ushmm.org.

2 Bonomolo and Kirchgaessner, "U.N. Says 800 Migrants Dead."

3 Kingsley, "More than 700 Migrants Feared Dead."

4 Missing Migrants Project.

Voluntary repatriation, or assisting refugees to return to their countries of origin, is viewed as the most ideal durable solution to reducing displacement.

Local integration means naturalization of refugees into their country of asylum.

Resettlement into a second or third host country is a protection tool for refugees who are unable or unwilling to return to their country of origin.

Refugees and asylum seekers encounter barriers to all three durable solutions. Even if a refugee were repatriated, it is back to a home that has been devastated by war, a place that is at once familiar and unfamiliar. And while it may seem from the news media that refugees are being easily resettled in hordes into the US, the truth is only about 1 percent of all refugees globally in any given year are resettled in a third country.

Some refugees who really need protection have a difficult time seeking asylum because of the unpredictable and chaotic nature of forced migration. Many refugees are either ignorant of asylum laws or are erroneously warned to go into hiding for fear of immediate deportation. Upon arrival, asylum seekers must prove to an asylum officer that they have "credible fear" of persecution and for that reason are seeking refuge in the US. If no case for credible fear can be made, they are deported. If they are allowed to stay, they may be held like a prisoner in a detention center with convicted criminals for months or years until they can make claim in front of a judge, a process which can be very subjective. The poor treatment and conditions in these jails often re-traumatize asylum seekers.

Women and children are especially at risk. Women and children make up the majority of the world's refugees and IDPs. Half of global refugees are children, many of them unaccompanied or separated. Women and children are more susceptible to forms of gender-based violence and discrimination, such as human trafficking, theft, extreme poverty, sexual assault, and lack of education and health care.

MY BROTHER'S KEEPER?

Burden sharing has been a long-standing issue in the refugee protection regime. Currently the United States is the top receiving country of refugees for resettlement. While the US contributes to alleviating the refugee crisis by being the top resettlement country, most of the hosting (temporary housing that can become long-term) is shouldered by developing countries, even some of the world's *least* developed countries. In the past few years Europe has been inundated with asylum seekers fleeing the Middle East and Central Asia. In a controversial move, Germany took in 1.1 million asylum seekers in just one year, 2015, sparking intense debate over how to manage the migrant crisis.[5]

---

5 Donahue and Delfs, "Germany Saw 1.1 Million Migrants."

UNHCR considers it vital for industrialized states to shoulder a larger portion of the refugee crisis, as safeguards to asylum are less stable in developing countries. The US has historically received the highest total number and percentage of refugees for resettlement of any country in the world. Other countries that have resettled large numbers of refugees include Canada, Australia, Norway, Germany, and Sweden.

What are your concerns, if any, about refugee resettlement and national security? Evaluate whether it is wise international policy to give refugees legal, permanent status.

What are your concerns, if any, about refugees taking away jobs from locals? About refugees changing the local culture?

THE VETTING PROCESS

One of the major controversies surrounding the refugee debate has to do with national security concerns, that by welcoming refugees our government ends up facilitating avenues for terrorism to slip in. This could not be farther from the truth. In fact, refugees are the most strictly screened immigrant group to enter the US. Here is the truth regarding the vetting process for refugees:[6]

- Vetting is an extensive and lengthy process.
- Refugees are security screened by several different agencies.
- Refugees are also health screened for contagious diseases.
- Refugees do not get to choose where they are resettled.
- Less than 1 percent of the global refugee population is ultimately approved for resettlement.

A refugee's first point of contact is with UNHCR, who determines where to resettle refugees based on presence of family members and other factors. Under the guidance of the US Department of State's Bureau of Population, Refugees, and Migrants, an in-country Resettlement Support Center (RSC) conducts initial interviews with refugees slotted for the US. They are then

---

6 US Citizenship and Immigration Services, "Refugee Processing and Security Screening."

vetted by several governmental entities: the Departments of State, Homeland Security, and Defense; the National Counterterrorism Center; and the FBI's Terrorist Screening Center. After approval by the US Citizenship and Immigration Services (USCIS) and passing a health screening, refugees are almost ready for departure. They must complete a cultural orientation, secure sponsorship assurances from a refugee agency in the US, and finally are referred to the International Organization for Migration (IOM) to make travel arrangements. Refugees sign a promissory note to repay their travel fees—on an interest-free loan—within forty-six months after arrival in the US. The entire process takes on average 18–24 months from initial application submission.[7]

> "The world will not be destroyed by those who do evil, but by those who watch them without doing anything."   —Albert Einstein

These facts should allay fears and clear up misconceptions surrounding the stringency of refugee admissions. As you can see, a terrorist trying to enter the US through a resettlement program has chosen a rather cumbersome pathway.

KNOWLEDGE LEADS TO ACTION

Refugees are too often seen as criminals, rather than victims of the worst circumstances. Our perceptions of refugees have long shaped our national policy towards admissions and resettlement. America, while being in many ways a welcoming nation, was slow to sign on to the UN refugee regime, as we'll learn in the next chapter. It is too easy to sympathize with the plight of refugees for a moment, only to soon forget about them. Geographical distance makes their struggle feel like "that" problem "over there." Bombardment by news media results in "compassion fatigue." Yet if we focus on their humanity and put ourselves in their shoes as fellow sojourners, it is easier to respond to the refugee crisis with compassion and generosity. Ordinary citizens can be a vessel of grace through small acts of kindness and hospitality. Former US Special Representative for Religion and Global Affairs Shaun Casey has stated:

> Despite the negative anti-refugee rhetoric that has been prevalent in US media and political discourse recently, many local refugee resettlement offices report that they continue to receive an outpouring of support from community members. It is innovative, "whole of society" collaboration and support at the local level—from religious leaders and communities, non-governmental organizations, social service providers, schools, police departments, municipal government leaders, and individual volunteers—that continues to make the refugee resettlement process possible and successful.[8]

---

7 The vast majority of refugees are able to pay back their loans within forty-six months. While it might seem harsh to expect them to pay back their travel loans, the repayment is what helps the US continue to assist other refugees.

8 Personal email exchange with Office of Religion and Global Affairs, US Department of State, December 1, 2016.

You've just absorbed a lot of information about the refugee crisis, but knowledge alone is not enough to make a difference. Making a difference requires action. The next chapter looks at the history of refugees in the United States. Chapter 6 and the Personal Action Plan will challenge you to get involved in your local context and beyond.

The Boatman

We were thirty-one souls all, he said, on the gray-sick of sea

in a cold rubber boat, rising and falling in our filth.

By morning this didn't matter, no land was in sight,

all were soaked to the bone, living and dead.

We could still float, we said, from war to war.

What lay behind us but ruins of stone piled on ruins of stone?

City called "mother of the poor" surrounded by fields

of cotton and millet, city of jewelers and cloak-makers,

with the oldest church in Christendom and the Sword of Allah.

If anyone remains there now, he assures, they would be utterly alone.

There is a hotel named for it in Rome two hundred meters

from the Piazza di Spagna, where you can have breakfast under

the portraits of film stars. There the staff cannot do enough for you.

But I am talking nonsense again, as I have since that night

we fetched a child, not ours, from the sea, drifting face-

down in a life vest, its eyes taken by fish or the birds above us.

After that, Aleppo went up in smoke, and Raqqa came under a rain

of leaflets warning everyone to go. Leave, yes, but go where?

We lived through the Americans and Russians, through Americans

again, many nights of death from the clouds, mornings surprised

to be waking from the sleep of death, still unburied and alive

but with no safe place. Leave, yes, we obey the leaflets, but go where?

To the sea to be eaten, to the shores of Europe to be caged?

To camp misery and camp remain here. I ask you then, where?

You tell me you are a poet. If so, our destination is the same.

I find myself now the boatman, driving a taxi at the end of the world.

I will see that you arrive safely, my friend, I will get you there.[9]

---

9 Forché, "The Boatman." Inspired by the Syrian refugee crisis and used with permission by poet.

REFLECTION QUESTIONS

1. Reflect on whether the US—one of the world's most developed and wealthiest nations—has a moral obligation to admit refugees today.

2. After reviewing the vetting process for refugees, how do you feel about welcoming refugees in our country?

3. In your opinion, are refugees a "burden" to society? Share your honest thoughts.

4. Describe a time when you received significant help from someone else during a time of need. What were the circumstances and how did it turn out? Now describe a time when you received comfort or encouragement from the Lord during a difficult season.

5. Where are you feeling challenged most as you go through this study? What perspective has shifted for you, either positively or negatively?

Spiritual Practice: Journaling

Journaling is a helpful way to process thoughts and emotions. Whether or not you have a habit of journaling, I invite you to write or verbally record your thoughts to this prompt:

Put yourself in the shoes of a refugee fleeing civil war. Engage your senses and imagine what you are seeing, hearing, tasting, smelling.

What is your heart feeling? What are your concerns as you leave your home, your city, your friends? What will you miss the most? The purpose of this exercise is not to sensationalize suffering but to develop compassion for the plight of refugees. When you are done, pray and ask God to help you love those who are fleeing for their lives.

Chapter 5

ALL THE WORLD IS HERE

But, though the conflict prove severe,
Let pilgrims resolute be found;
For succor will, at length, appear,
And they with vict'ry shall be crown'd.

–John Bunyan, The Pilgrim's Progress

BEFORE WE BEGIN

Chapter 5 reflects upon our nation's history of refugee welcome, the current makeup of arrivals, and what implications this has for us who follow Jesus.

Unless you belong to an American indigenous people, you have an immigrant heritage. Write down how and when your family came to the US.

In what ways does your immigrant heritage (if applicable) impact your identity and self-understanding?

Massachusetts has a rich history of refugees, going back several centuries to America's original refugees, whom we call "Pilgrims." The Pilgrims came to America to establish free communities of worship, landing at Plymouth Harbor, Massachusetts, in 1620.

In the early 1800s visionaries grew a booming textile industry in Lowell, Massachusetts, later dubbed the "Cradle of the American Industrial Revolution." The area began welcoming European immigrants to grow the economy. However, the southward shift of the national textile industry in the 1920s and the Great Depression of the 1930s hit Lowell hard, and its economy flattened. The historic mill town of Lowell withered to just a shadow of its earlier glory days.

Then in the 1970s, the Khmer Rouge instigated a genocide in Cambodia, leading to the death and displacement of millions of Cambodians. A large number were resettled in Lowell. The high-tech boom of that decade and the decision of Wang Laboratories to build their world headquarters in Lowell created low-wage computer assembly jobs requiring low skills and no English. Refugees settled there were able to find jobs.

There was a significant secondary migration to Lowell as more Cambodians reconnected with long-lost family and friends. Since 1980, refugee resettlement and immigration have drastically impacted Lowell. In 1980 the ethnic minority population was less than 5 percent; thirty years later, non-whites represented 30 percent of the city. Between 1980 and 2000, the Asian population alone increased by an astonishing 2,876 percent![1] Most of Lowell's Asian population is Cambodian. In fact, Lowell boasts the second largest Cambodian population in America (the first is Long Beach, California).[2]

Today, Lowell is one of the most ethnically diverse cities in Massachusetts, with Asians constituting 22.3 percent of its population.[3] Through the assistance of non-profit organizations like the International Institute of Lowell and the Cambodian Mutual Assistance Association, the Cambodian refugee population has been able to establish a thriving community in this New England town that not so long ago was flailing in recession.

WHO'S COMING TO AMERICA?

In the aftermath of World War II, the United States took in hundreds of thousands of Europeans who had been displaced by the war. In total, over 650,000 refugees were admitted following the enactment of the Displaced Persons Act of 1948. But America initially withheld from signing the 1951 Refugee Convention because it did not reflect our ideological stance against Communism. It was not until 1965 that the new Immigration and Nationality Act increased quotas of immigrants from non-European nations. Refugee admissions, however, were not greatly impacted by it. The 1980 Refugee Reform Act created the Office of Refugee Resettlement, and the US increased yearly caps, finally complying with the 1967 Protocol.

---

1 Donico, "Cambodian Americans."

2 Cambodian Mutual Assistance Association.

3 University of Massachusetts, "Population of Asian Americans."

Refugee admissions are affected by several factors. World events, politics, racial attitudes, public sympathy, and political atmosphere all play into admission decisions, but least of all is personal preference of refugees. However, refugees are often resettled where they can maintain cultural ties and reunite with family and friends. The resettlement of refugees to an area can have significant impact on its cultural, economic, and demographic identity.

What do you know about the demographic makeup of your neighborhood or city?

What kind of changes, if any, has immigration made in your area over the past twenty years? The past five? Do you view these changes as generally positive or negative?

Refugee Arrivals

Since 1975, the US has resettled over three million refugees.[4] Each year, the president of the United States, after consulting with Congress, sets an admissions ceiling on how many refugees will be accepted for resettlement from different regions of the world. The graph below compares annual ceiling numbers against actual number of admitted refugees.[5] The lines tend to stay close until the early 2000s, the most noticeable gap being the dip in refugee admissions following the 9/11 attacks in 2001 (but the admissions ceiling was still set at 70,000 for 2002). An increase in concern around national security has impacted refugee admissions until present day. The refugee admissions ceiling and actual

9/11 and Refugee Admissions

Following the September 11, 2001, attacks on the World Trade Center in New York City, refugee admissions were temporarily halted as the nation reassessed its security plans regarding admitting foreigners. In 1990, the US admitted 122,000 refugees; in 2002 only 27,110 were admitted, a 25-yr low. Since 2004, the numbers have steadily increased but are still lower than they were in the 1980s and 90s.

— US Dept of State, Bureau of Populations, Refugees and Migration (PRM): 2009

---

4 Data searchable at Refugee Processing Center data, www.wrapsnet.org.

5 Migration Policy Institute, "US Annual Refugee Resettlement Ceilings." You can visit the Refugee Processing Center website (https://www.wrapsnet.org/admissions-and-arrivals/) to pull up historical refugee admissions reports. It's easy and kind of fun.

admissions hit historic lows during the Trump administration (2017–2020) when our historically bipartisan attitude towards resettlement faced political polarization exacerbated by coronavirus concerns.

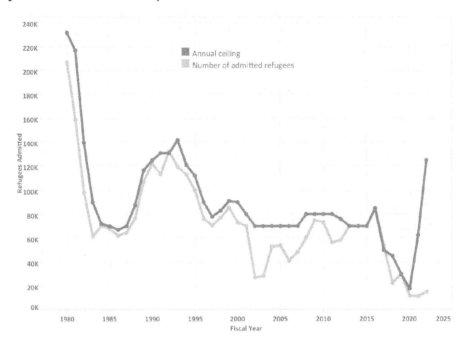

Figure 1 US Refugee Admissions & Refugee Resettlement Ceilings, FY 1980–2022 (thru June 2022)
Migration Policy Institute Data Hub

While Muslim refugees are dominating the news these days, many Americans do not realize that the majority of refugees accepted by America have historically been Christian, especially before 2020.[6] This includes Burmese and Bhutanese minority Christian groups, Orthodox Christian Iraqis, and thousands of Christians from eastern Africa, many of whom were persecuted in their home countries. These are, therefore, our persecuted brothers and sisters in Christ, and they come as a prophetic voice and blessing to the church in America.

Today independent immigrant churches are the fastest growing among evangelical churches in the US.[7] The Catholic church in America, of which 25 percent were born outside of the country, is bolstered by, if not dependent upon, the presence of immigrants and refugees for their revitalization.[8] So Christian refugees are not just our guests, they are our family. They are changing the landscape, not just of our nation, but also of our churches.

---

6 Data searchable at Refugee Processing Center data, www.wrapsnet.org.

7 Johnson, "USA Evangelicals/Evangelicals in a Global Context."

8 Gjelten and Peñaloza, "Built by Immigrants."

How do you feel about the increasing numbers of Muslim refugees being resettled in the US?

Is there a particular group of refugees or immigrants which cause you the most concern? Why?

The Nations Have Come

International policy can facilitate the entry of refugees into our country, but once they are here, it is resettlement agencies and concerned citizens who make a difference in how well refugees integrate. Nine different nonprofit agencies help refugees settle in the US. (See Appendix A for a complete list.) The agencies help refugees find housing and jobs, but they also highly depend on volunteers to assist with the resettlement process, from setting up apartments to teaching ESL to enrolling kids in school.

> We, the community of faith, are judged by the way we treat the most vulnerable among us... Our church communities must find pastoral and legal ways to welcome our brothers and sisters in faith.
> —"Strangers No Longer," Catholic document on migration

The nations have come to America, creating a tremendous opportunity for us to live out our faith and commitment to Christ. Yet in a 2016 Lifeway survey, pastors revealed that their churches have a sense of fear about refugees coming to the US (46%) and some (13%) did not believe Christians have a responsibility to care sacrificially for refugees and foreigners.[9] Furthermore, lack of education about geography and global events only compounds fear of the unknown. It takes a lot of commitment to keeping up with the news to understand why Ukrainians are at the Mexican border, or why we have both Iranian Muslims and Iranian Christians flying in from Papua New Guinea, or to know that Afghanistan is not in the Middle East.

In our final chapter, we will look at hospitality narratives in the Bible. Today, the ends of the earth are coming to America, and you have the opportunity to show them God's love without having to leave your home. The last words of Jesus before his Ascension were, "But you will receive power when the Holy Spirit has

---

9 Chandler, "To Love, not Fear."

come upon you, and you will be my witnesses in Jerusalem and in all Judea and Samaria and to the end of the earth" (Acts 1:8). How will you respond to the refugees in your midst? What is your vision for making the most of this opportunity?

> We distinguish that the refugees fleeing this violence are not our enemies; they are victims. We call for Christians to support ministries showing the love of Jesus to the most vulnerable, those in desperate need, and the hurting. This is what Jesus did; He came to the hurting and brought peace to those in despair.
>
> Critical moments like these are opportunities for us to be like Jesus, showing and sharing His love to the hurting and the vulnerable in the midst of this global crisis. Thus we declare that we care, we are responding because our allegiance is to Jesus, and we seek to be more like Him, emulating His compassionate care for the most vulnerable.[10]

REFLECTION QUESTIONS

1. Recall the five categories of persecution that define "refugee" according to the United Nations. Make a list of any biblical characters who were persecuted based on one of those categories.

2. Would you advocate for more or fewer refugees being settled in our country? In your city? Why or why not?

---

10 GC2 Summit Statement, "Christian Declaration on Caring for Refugees."

3. Why is making yourself knowledgeable about a refugee's background so crucial?

4. With continuing immigration into the United States, how can Christians in America view this as an opportunity to live out their faith?

5. Stop and say a prayer for the persecuted global church. See Open Doors USA's World Watch List for guidance on how to pray (https://www.opendoorsusa.org/christian-persecution/world-watch-list/).

Spiritual Practice: Worship

The nations are coming to America, and many are Christians whose faith has been tested by the fire of persecution. Revelation 7 paints a picture of every tribe and tongue worshiping before the Lord's throne:

> After this I looked, and there before me was a great multitude that no one could count, from every nation, tribe, people and language, standing before the throne and before the Lamb. They were wearing white robes and were holding palm branches in their hands. And they cried out in a loud voice:
>
> > "Salvation belongs to our God,
> > who sits on the throne,
> > and to the Lamb." (Rev 7:9-10 NIV)

Using a music app or YouTube, do a search for worship in a language you don't speak (for instance, you can type "Persian worship" or "Swahili worship" into the search bar in Spotify). For ten minutes, listen to songs in that language and imagine yourself worshiping with someone from that background. Try to appreciate the songs without judging their quality or melody. Use your holy imagination to envision people from every nation, tribe, people, and language standing before the throne and before the Lamb in worship!

Chapter 6

SERVING ANGELS

"Faith in God's love toward man is perfected in man's love to God and neighbor." –H. Richard Niebuhr

BEFORE WE BEGIN

Our final chapter will look at the role of hospitality in the redemption narrative of Scripture and how it applies to us today in regard to refugees.

Recall a time when you received another's generosity or hospitality. What type of impression did it leave on you?

What does hospitality look like in your home? In what ways can you envision yourself offering hospitality to refugees, whether inside or outside of your home?

Imagine you are at seated at a rich banquet table. The linen is freshly pressed and silky to the touch. Food overflows the silver platters, and the air is sweet with the aroma of wine. A melodic tune plays overhead while graceful servers delicately spoon the meal onto your plate. The food is exquisite, the service impeccable. This is a meal you can never repay, for the host cannot be repaid. He is too great and too generous.

Most [evangelical Christians] see newcomers as a threat or a burden. Only 4 in 10 see a gospel opportunity.

—Matthew Soerens, World Relief

This is what it is like at the Lord's Table. At the Lord's Table, the Lord is the divine host who opens his home and provides for his people. We live by God's invitation and in his favor (Lev 25:23; Ps 15:1; 39:12; Matt 22:1–14).[1] As God's ambassadors, Christians reflect God's hospitality to the stranger when we turn and practice hospitality as a fruit of our faith. These verses point out the significance of hospitality to our Christian ethic:

- "Show hospitality to one another without grumbling" (1 Pet 4:9).

- "Contribute to the needs of the saints and seek to show hospitality" (Rom 12:13).

- "Do not neglect to show hospitality to strangers … Do not neglect to do good and to share what you have, for such sacrifices are pleasing to God" (Heb 13:2, 16).

- "Bear one another's burdens, and so fulfill the law of Christ" (Gal 6:1).

- "So then, as we have opportunity, let us do good to everyone, and especially to those who are of the household of faith" (Gal 6:10).

- "Beloved, it is a faithful thing you do in all your efforts for these brothers, strangers as they are …" (3 John 5).

THE ROLE OF HOSPITALITY IN THE REDEMPTION NARRATIVE

In Genesis chapter 18, Abraham is sitting by the oaks of Mamre, resting in the doorway of his tent during the heat of the day. Three men appear to him, and he immediately rushes to provide them with sustenance: water to wash up and bread, curds, wheat cakes, and choice meat to eat. As a foreigner himself, Abraham was eager to welcome other sojourners.

Abraham thought he was entertaining men, but in reality he was offering hospitality to the Lord himself. The three strangers, who are soon revealed as angelic messengers from God, bring Abraham good news of Sarah's promised conception. Abraham's story reminds us not to let opportunities to show hospitality pass us by.[2] "Do not neglect to show hospitality to strangers, for thereby some have entertained angels unawares," we read in Hebrews 13:2.

Other biblical examples of hospitality in a redemptive role include:

- Elijah at Zarephath: God commanded the widow to provide for him and God in return sustained their food supply (1 Kgs 17).

---

1 Buttrick, *Interpreter's Dictionary of the Bible*, 399.

2 See Appendix E for how this biblical story has inspired this book.

- Ruth in Bethlehem: Boaz ensured that Ruth and Naomi received a generous share of the harvest (Ruth 2).

- Elisha in Shunem: a Gentile woman provided food and residence for Elisha because he was a prophet of God. God blessed her with a son and her land was restored to her after she was forced to sojourn in Philistine during a famine (2 Kgs 4, 8).

- The man of Ephraim sojourning in Gibeah: the old farmer took care of all his needs (Judg 19).

- Zacchaeus, the tax collector: Jesus was passing through Jericho and invited himself to the home of Zacchaeus (Luke 19). Zaccheus repented of his fraud and repaid anyone he had wronged fourfold.

- Jesus in Samaria: after the Samaritan woman at the well believed in Jesus, the Samaritans invited Jesus to stay with them for two days (John 4).

- The Good Samaritan: he cared for all the needs of the injured man (Luke 10).

- Lydia in Philippi: after her baptism she provided for Paul and his companions on their missionary journey (Acts 16).

When we, like the examples above, welcome the stranger, we not only act out our faith, but we also minister on behalf of Christ:

> For he himself is our peace, who has made us both one and has broken down his flesh the dividing wall of hostility.
>
> —Ephesians 2:14

> Then the King will say to those on his right, "Come, you who are blessed by my Father, inherit the kingdom prepared for you from the foundation of the world. For I was hungry and you gave me food, I was thirsty and you gave me drink, I was a stranger and you welcomed me, I was naked and you clothed me, I was sick and you visited me, I was in prison and you came to me."
>
> Then the righteous will answer him, saying, "Lord, when did we see you hungry and feed you, or thirsty and give you drink? And when did we see you a stranger and welcome you, or naked and clothe you? And when did we see you sick or in prison and visit you?"
>
> And the King will answer them, "Truly, I say to you, as you did it to one of the least of these my brothers, you did it to me" (Matt 25:34–40).

Name at least one biblical basis for practicing hospitality:

How does hospitality reflect God's character through us?

From Hardship to Hardship

No one will dispute the contributions to American society, science, education, politics, and literature made by the likes of scientist Albert Einstein, statesman Henry Kissinger, stateswoman Madeleine Albright, the Von Trapp family of "Sound of Music" fame, singer Gloria Estefan, author Isabel Allende, or Nobel Prize-winning writers Alexander Solzhenitsyn and Elie Wiesel. What these luminaries have in common is that they were refugees. The grit and perseverance that helped them survive their flight are the same qualities that helped them thrive in their new lives.

But rebuilding is difficult. Globalization has created a myriad of unanticipated narrative arcs. The nationality listed on a refugee's visa doesn't always indicate country of birth or residence. Because conflict forces refugees from their homes, refugees—especially children and youth—may not have ever lived in the country listed as their nationality, thus creating identity ambiguity. Then, upon arrival, refugees are thrust into rebuilding their lives in another new culture, system, and language. Many suffer from PTSD, culture shock, and exhaustion. Many develop depression. While refugees are grateful to be resettled in the States, many feel so lost here they would prefer to return to their camp or even to their home country. While that might seem incredulous to us, we must have empathy and patience with those who are trying to rebuild everything that was lost to them. The sense of lost identity and meaning takes a huge emotional toll.

For a minority of refugees, resettlement is still the best durable solution chosen for them. Since 1975 the US has made room for almost 3.5 million refugees, settled in 180 cities.[3] Over the past decade states like Texas, California, and New York have historically taken in the most refugees, but in recent years states like Kentucky and Washington have taken in higher numbers of arrivals than you might expect; over the past decade Idaho, a less populated state, has taken in refugees per capita.[4]

One of the goals of resettlement is to help refugees become independent and self-sustaining. Refugees receive government-provided short-term cash and medical assistance; they also receive case management, employment services, English courses, and civics instruction. The refugees' visa status authorizes them to work, and after one year, refugees are eligible for Lawful Permanent Resident status, also known as a "green card." Five years after that, they can become US citizens.

While refugees do receive government assistance, it is barely enough to get their feet off the ground. Depending on what type of assistance program they are on, the benefits can provide up to eight months of support. While that is helpful, eight months is rarely enough time to be truly "self-sustainable." Churches and welcoming citizens can stand in the gap when policy is not enough. Seminary professor Christine Pohl writes:

---

3 Data searchable at Refugee Processing Center data, www.wrapsnet.org.

4 See Radford, "Just 10 states."

Reception of refugees is one of the few places in modern politics where the explicit language of hospitality is still used. People continue to connect theological notions of sanctuary, cities of refuge, and care for aliens with the needs of today's displaced people. Christians have a vital role in making sure that the needs of refugees are taken seriously by national governments. But our response must extend beyond public policy to more personal involvement in voluntary agencies, communities, churches, and homes where acts of welcome offer refuge and new life to some of the world's most vulnerable people.[5]

Refugees come to America having lost almost everything: family, friends, home, material comforts, money. But they are survivors. Refugees inspire us because they have encountered tremendous hardship with resilience and resourcefulness.

Ways to Care for Refugees

We're heading into the practical section of the workbook, where you will brainstorm how to get into action and extend a welcome to refugees. Before we look at your Personal Action Plan, here's a list of ideas:

> And whoever gives one of these little ones even a cup of cold water because he is a disciple, truly, I say to you, he will be no means lose his reward.
>
> —Matthew 10:42

- **Connect.** Identify the refugee resettlement agencies in your city and explore the volunteer opportunities they offer.

- **Prepare a warm welcome.** Collect furniture and household goods for their apartment and help them settle in when they arrive or move to their permanent housing. Prepare welcome kits of basic necessities or arrange for meals to be delivered during their first week.

- **Invite them into your home.** Offer to host a refugee family who is awaiting permanent housing. Invite them to share a meal. Friendships are formed over food but be sure to educate yourself about the refugee family's cultural background. Do not serve foods that would be considered unclean, non-kosher, or offensive to them. Know what "halal" means. Learn about their table culture and mannerisms.

- **Find their "home away from home."** Try to connect refugees with people from their countries of origin. The sense of community and familiarity of language and culture will be of great comfort.

- **Find common ground.** Activities that communicate warmth and friendship but do not require much language fluency are a good starting place. Play soccer, play simple card and board games, visit a park, or cook together.

---

5 Pohl, *Making Room*, 166.

- **Take them shopping.** Accompany your refugee friends to the grocery store. While you're shopping you can teach them food vocabulary and how to make good selections. Afterwards, you could shows them how to cook American dishes. Show them where to buy inexpensive household products.

- **Help prepare their children for school and new friends.** Children do not have the developed coping mechanisms of adults and may struggle to understand their situation. Most new arrivals will be concerned about their children's integration into a new school system and new peer circles. Registering their children for school, learning bus routes, and purchasing school supplies is a daunting task and an area where locals can provide a lot of help.

- **Teach them English.** This is possibly the most helpful tool you can give refugees who do not already know English. Teach them slang. Introduce them to the public library and to quality television programs. If they have young children, the children will likely learn English very quickly in school and will soon be able to help translate for their parents. However, in order for the adults to be empowered and equipped to work, it is essential that they, too, master English.

- **Help them get mobile.** Teach them how to drive a car, where to buy a bike, how to ride the bus or subway, how to read a map. Mobility is important to achieving independence.

- **Be a good listener.** Refugees have stories of hardship, struggle, and loss. Many suffer from PTSD and need counseling. Be a part of the healing process by lending an ear to their stories. Unless you are a trained counselor, refrain from giving psychological advice, as you might end up doing more harm than good.

- **Celebrate the holidays together.** Find out what holidays or holy days are special in your refugee friend's home country; include them in celebrating American holidays.

- **Help them find a place of worship.** Finding a community of faith will provide a safety network and support system. Be sensitive about honoring their religion, regardless of whether they are open to your Christian faith. Do not make conversion the basis of your friendship. Sharing about each other's faith is appropriate, but remember newcomers are in a vulnerable position and may feel pressured to agree with you for the sake of your assistance and relationship.

- **Pray for them.** Ask God to open your heart to refugees. Pray for the healing of their trauma and for their integration to a new country and culture. Pray that God would open their hearts to Himself.

- **Ask them for help or advice.** You read that right. Friendship is mutual, and refugees feel respected and valued when they can offer you something back. Resist the "savior complex" and look upon your refugee friends as being capable of teaching you something you didn't know. Avoid behaving like their benefactor.

- **Advocate for refugees.** Raise your voice to speak for the voiceless and powerless. By lifting up a prophetic voice, Christians can nurture a moral public ethos of hospitality toward the stranger. Contact your national congressional representatives and local politicians. You can start here: http://www.whoismyrepresentative.com/.

- **Host a Refugee Sunday.** Make refugees the focus of one Sunday at your church; Refugee Sundays are often held in June to coincide with World Refugee Day, June 20. For ideas, see worldrelief.org/refugee-sunday/.

- **Read refugee memoirs and watch refugee documentaries.** These will open your eyes to the experiences of refugees and make you more knowledgeable, culturally sensitive, and compassionate. Reading a book or watching a film with friends will provide a forum for conversation. See Appendix B and the Bibliography for ideas.

- Most of all, **be a friend**! Be available to refugees and invite them into your life. Don't try to fix all their problems—show the love of Christ to refugees by caring for them as friends.

Which of these ideas can you see yourself taking on? What would be the first step to turning it into an action item?

THE LEAST OF THESE

A doctrine of hospitality should inform the way we view government policies that impact refugees. Refugees have a compelling case for hospitality and mercy. When we view the world through the lens of our narrative faith, we come to realize that we have often let patriotism override faith. God, forgive us for that. The Church in America has been blessed in many ways. We are a numerically large and

Conversion to God, therefore, means a simultaneous conversion to the other persons who live with you on this earth. The farmer, the worker, the student, the prisoner, the sick, the black, the white, the weak, the strong, the oppressed and the oppressor, the patient and the one who heals, the tortured and the torturer, the boss and the flunky, not only are they people like you, but they are also called to make themselves heard and to give God a chance to be the God of all.

–Henri Nouwen, *With Open Hands*, 114

materially wealthy member of the global Body of Christ, with many resources at our disposal. But those resources are not simply for us to enjoy—we have a moral obligation to share with "the least of these," as unto Christ himself. Jesus said, "And whoever gives one of these little ones even a cup of cold water because he is a disciple, truly, I say to you, he will be no means lose his reward" (Matt 10:42). He also said, "Everyone to whom much was given, of him much will be required, and from him to whom they entrusted much, they will demand the more" (Luke 12:48).

No matter where you stand on the refugee debate, it will not change the reality that refugees have come to our country. Some are thriving, some are barely surviving. Scripture commands hospitality to the stranger. We experience God through hospitality offered to strangers. This spiritual reality challenges us to view refugees not as a burden, but as an asset to our communities, and to view immigration issues as also moral issues, not just economic and political ones. Think of the impact the church in America could have in providing far-reaching assistance and displaying gospel-rooted love to people from all over the world, for the sake of the kingdom. With the world in our backyard, we have a unique opportunity to welcome the stranger. Jesus loved radically. Let us be radical in the way we fulfill the hospitality-driven, justice-laden mission of God.

PERSONAL REFLECTION

1. How have you seen your church address immigration or discrimination in recent years? In what areas would you like to see it grow cross-culturally?

2. Henri Nouwen said we must be converted to one another. What do you think he meant by this? What thoughts or feelings of yours need to be converted?

3. What could you learn from refugees? List all the ways in which they could be an asset or blessing to you personally or to your community.

4. What lingering questions do you have after reading through this study? Consider doing your own research online, through the library, or through a refugee advocacy organization to find the answers. (See Appendix B.)

5. Take some time now to pray for refugees, for their protection, safety, and the rebuilding of their lives. Pray that God would move in the hearts of his people to welcome refugees with generosity, compassion, and mercy.

Spiritual Practice: Hospitality

The Greek word for hospitality is *philoxenia*, which means "love of strangers." In modern practice, hospitality is usually reserved for friends and acquaintances and can be transactional, with each party taking turns hosting. In biblical times, however, hospitality, even to total strangers, was an honor-bound duty. Hosting a weary traveler passing through a village in need of a place to stay the night would not be an uncommon scenario.

For this final spiritual practice, extend hospitality to someone you do not normally spend a lot of time with. Invite them to your home, treat them to coffee, suggest a walk … whatever you feel comfortable doing. As the host, expect nothing back from the other person. Be a good listener, minimize distractions to give your undivided attention, and try to see your guest as a person made in the image of God.

Afterwards, reflect upon your time together. Journal about it.

Were you able to give full attention to the other person?

What did you learn about them?

What did you learn about yourself?

Where did you see God at work during your time together?

CONCLUSION

Once I thought to write a history of the immigrants in America.
Then I discovered that the immigrants were American history.
—Oscar Handlin

At the beginning of this study, you met Mariane from Rwanda. After US approval for resettlement, Mariane's family arrived in Houston in 1997. They knew no one and spoke no English, so the transition was extremely difficult. Resolved to become independent, both Mariane and her husband enrolled in school to learn English. Mariane eventually found her way into the hotel industry. She was well-received there due to the global outlook of the industry. She worked her way up from housekeeping, eventually landing a managerial role in accounting, where she still works today. Meanwhile her husband was able to earn his MS in Engineering, and he, too, was promoted to manager. Gradually the family started to find stability in their new lives.

Although she still aches for Rwanda, Mariane is able to say she feels "happy" because she can see the fruit of her trials: "What doesn't break you makes you stronger. I feel like I have found myself again." Mariane encourages recently arrived refugees to embrace the best of what America has to offer, beginning with education. She says, "People have many freedoms here and hard work pays off. Close the door behind you and open another one. You don't have to live in between doors."

For Mariane, the hardest part about continuing her life in the United States is being without her family, most of whom still live in Rwanda. "No human being would prefer losing her beloved country and being called a 'refugee.' Everyone would definitely return home if they could, but that opportunity has not knocked at my door as of yet," she says. Mariane visited her country in 2004 and would like to retire there someday. For now, her goal is to mentor refugees and help them obtain an education and become independent, as she and her husband have been able to achieve.

"THE NEW COLOSSUS"

The Statue of Liberty is *the* iconic symbol of freedom and of the United States of America. Standing gracefully on Liberty Island in New York Harbor, she has welcomed millions of immigrants, both during the period (1892 to 1954) when the site served as the nation's busiest immigrant inspection station to the present day as a national monument and tourist attraction. Designed by Frédéric Bartholdi, the statue was presented as a gift from France and dedicated in 1886. The Lady represents Libertas, the Roman goddess of freedom, at whose feet lies a broken chain. Her arms bear a torch and a *tabula ansata* (a tablet evoking the concept of law) upon which is inscribed in Roman numerals 1776, the date of the Declaration of Independence.

Originally intended to represent international republicanism, the Statue of Liberty has come to be viewed instead as the welcoming mother—the symbol of America's immigration history. So many immigrants have sailed by her that as many as 40 percent of Americans can trace their roots to Ellis Island.[1] Engraved on a plaque mounted on the statue's pedestal is the poem, "The New Colossus":

Not like the brazen giant of Greek fame,

With conquering limbs astride from land to land;

Here at our sea-washed, sunset gates shall stand

A mighty woman with a torch, whose flame

Is the imprisoned lightning, and her name

Mother of Exiles. From her beacon-hand

Glows world-wide welcome; her mild eyes command

The air-bridged harbor that twin cities frame.

"Keep, ancient lands, your storied pomp!" cries she

With silent lips. "Give me your tired, your poor,

Your huddled masses yearning to breathe free,

The wretched refuse of your teeming shore.

Send these, the homeless, tempest-tost to me,

I lift my lamp beside the golden door!"

This sonnet was penned by Jewish-American poet Emma Lazarus in 1883, so long ago, yet the words still reflect the American vision, a vision that today is being treated with contempt in so many corners of our nation. Our country was established on the backs of immigrants and refugees arriving tired, poor, and yearning to breathe free, just like those arriving on our doorstep today. They have suffered oppression and sadly, many continue to suffer it on our shores and at our doors.

Embracing refugees, the "huddled masses" in our midst, is more than an origin myth—it is our history. So much of America's relative prosperity is owed to the ingenuity and industry of our immigrant forebears. We are a "permanently unfinished nation," one whose story is changing at an ever-faster pace in increasing diversity, thanks to the globalized world we inhabit.[2]

---

1 Pipher, *Middle of Everywhere*, xxiii.

2 Bohmer and Shuman, *Rejecting Refugees*, 1.

Refugees are members of our vast global family, sharing in the same common humanity.[3] Refugees are like you and me, citizens of the world who have hopes and dreams and want to establish a good life for their families.

America is still a great land of opportunity—but we can do better. We can be a better country for newcomers to make a new home. We can do a better job sharing our resources. We can do better at embracing the nations that have come. The "American Dream" is not just about the opportunity to become a financial success story, but to live in a land that welcomes all peoples and "glows worldwide welcome."

Holocaust survivor Elie Wiesel praised the "righteous Gentiles" who risked their lives protecting the Jewish refugees. Many of those who rescued persecuted Jews during the Holocaust were of a different ethnic and religious background, yet they acted against their self-interest, driven by their belief in a common humanity. May we who follow Christ see the image of God in refugees and welcome and advocate for the least of these, as he commanded. Walking with uprooted people through the process of restoring their lives is an act of discipleship and a vicarious act of grace, for we, too, were once strangers. We, too, are looking for a better country.

Pray this litany aloud:

Their feet are tired and aching
Lord, have mercy on their soles
Their backs are hunched and breaking
Lord, have mercy on their souls
We see them there, but too afraid to act
Lord, have mercy on our souls
They fight and hope and pray and scrap
Lord, have mercy on their souls
They come from afar, we don't know their ways
Lord, help us to trust
We want to care, but it's hard to share
Lord, help us to give
They're made in your image, they're your children too
Lord, help us to love
We're called by faith beyond ourselves
Lord, help us to live
Lord, help us to see you in the face of
the sojourner | the wanderer | the shipwrecked
the lost boy | the widow | the orphan
the abandoned | the scorned | the displaced
THE REFUGEE.

---

3 For exploration of Christian identity and belonging to a global family, see Johnson and Wu, *Our Global Families*.

PERSONAL ACTION PLAN

"He has told you, O man, what is good; and what does the Lord require of you but to do justice, and to love kindness, and to walk humbly with your God?" Micah 6:8

You are invited to develop a Personal Action Plan. Your personal action plan will help you apply what you have learned through this study and take a first or farther step in caring for the refugees in your midst. While this plan is geared towards in-person involvement, even if you do not live in an area of the country with refugees, you can think creatively about getting involved somehow. Look back at the list of ideas in Chapter 6; you can also refer to Appendix B: A Refugee Resource List.

　　Follow the steps below to create a personal action plan. You can do this individually or with your group.

1. Pray and ask God to direct your plans. Ask him to give you sensitivity and wisdom as you discern how he's calling you to care for refugees. Express your fears about the unknowns.

2. Identify a particular refugee community or refugee agency within your city that you feel drawn to. I suggest you choose something close by to increase your chance of participation. To see what volunteer organizations are near you, scan the QR codes, or visit www.acf.hhs.gov/orr/map/find-resources-and-contacts-your-state. I also highly recommend USAHello.org. Write down your findings here:

3. What type of activity (or activities) do you feel would be realistic for you to take on? Write your notes here:

4. What is the date of your activity?

5. What supplies or provisions will you need for your action plan? Make a list here:

6. What expectations do you have of this action plan? If you have any qualms or concerns, write them here:

7. Do you have long-term or short-term vision for this action plan? If this is something that can be a repeated or regular commitment, write down thoughts on how to sustain it.

8. The plan you have designed should be realistic. Now, come up with a "stretch goal"—something that will require more commitment and faith, something you aspire to do.

9. Pray and commit your plans, time, and service to the Lord. Be willing to serve and care for refugees no matter the outcome. They might not have the language skills to show you their appreciation, but love them anyways.

Thank you for stepping out in faith to create this Personal Action Plan. Now it's your turn to challenge someone to do this study and get into action to care for refugees!

Appendix A

RESETTLEMENT AGENCIES

Nine national agencies resettle refugees in the United States. Search online to see if these agencies have an office in your city (https://www.acf.hhs.gov/orr/map/find-resources-and-contacts-your-state).

Church World Service (CWS)
475 Riverside Drive, Suite 700
New York, NY 10115-0050
Phone: (212) 870-2061
cwsglobal.org
irp@churchworldservice.org

Episcopal Migration Ministries (EMM)
815 Second Avenue
New York, NY 10017
Phone: 1-800-334-7626
episcopalmigrationministries.org
emm@episcopalchurch.org

Ethiopian Community Development Council (ECDC)
901 South Highland Street
Arlington, VA 22204
Phone: (703) 685-0510
www.ecdcus.org; info@edcdus.org

Hebrew Immigration Aid Society (HIAS)
1300 Spring Street, Suite 500
Silver Spring, MD 20910
Phone: 1-800-442-7714
hias.org; info@hias.org

International Rescue Committee (IRC)
122 East 42nd Street
New York, NY 10168
Phone: (212) 551-3000
rescue.org

Lutheran Immigration & Refugee Service (LIRS)
700 Light Street
Baltimore, MD 21230-3850
Phone: (410) 983-4000
lirs.org

US Committee for Refugees and Immigrants (USCRI)
2231 Crystal Drive, Suite 350
Arlington VA 22202-3711
Phone: (703) 310-1130
refugees.org
uscri@uscridc.org

US Conference of Catholic Bishops/Migration and Refugee Services (USCCB/MRS)
3211 Fourth Street, NE
Washington, DC 20017
Phone: (202) 541-3000
usccb.org

World Relief
7 East Baltimore Street
Baltimore, MD 21202
Phone: (443) 451-1900
worldrelief.org

Appendix B

A REFUGEE RESOURCE LIST

This appendix contains just a few examples of a variety of resources related to refugees.
I recommend doing your own internet search for the most recent publications and releases.

THE REFUGEE CRISIS AND IMMIGRATION

Baumer, Stephan, Matthew Soerens, and Issam Smeir. *Seeking Refuge: On the Shores of the Global Refugee Crisis*. Chicago: Moody Publishers, 2016.
Chapter 5 of this informative book provides details on the resettlement process and the role of agencies. The appendix contains this link to a map showing the locations of the major resettlement agencies in the US: http://bit.ly/RefugeeResettlementMap.

Carroll R., M. Daniel. *Christians at the Border: Immigration, the Church, and the Bible* (Second Edition). Grand Rapids: Baker Academic, 2013.
Currently one of the foremost scholars on the subject of Christian perspectives on immigration reform, Carroll explores whether immigrant influx should be viewed as an invasion or opportunity, grounding his positions on biblical principles.

Loescher, Gil, Alexander Betts, and James Milner. *The United Nations High Commissioner for Refugees (UNHCR): The Politics and Practice of Refugee Protection into the Twenty-First Century*. Global Institutions. London: Routledge, 2008.
A concise and comprehensive introduction to both the world of refugees and the UN organization that protects and assists them. Written by experts in the field, it traces the relationship between state interests, global politics, and the work of the UNHCR.

Soerens, Matthew, and Jenny Yang. *Welcoming the Stranger: Justice, Compassion & Truth in the Immigration Debate* (Revised and Expanded edition). Downers Grove: InterVarsity Press, 2018.
Soerens and Yang are immigration experts who work with World Relief, the humanitarian arm of the National Association of Evangelicals.

MEMOIRS AND INSPIRATIONAL STORIES

Ahmedi, Farah, with Tamim Ansary. *The Other Side of the Sky*. New York: Gallery, 2006.
An Afghan high school student's poignant memoir of her losses and gains as a refugee from Afghanistan to America.

Eggers, Dave. *What Is the What*. New York: Vintage, 2007.
The inspiring biography of a "Lost Boy of Sudan" who resettles in the United States, where he finds promise but also faces challenges and heartache.

Mosley, Don and Hollyday, Joyce. *Faith Beyond Borders: Doing Justice in a Dangerous World*. Nashville: Abingdon Press, 2010.
Don Mosley helped launch Habitat for Humanity and Jubilee Partners, a Christian service community that has welcomed thousands of refugees.

St. John, Warren. *Outcasts United: An American Town, a Refugee Team, and One Woman's Quest to Make a Difference*. New York: Random House, 2009.
The extraordinary tale of a refugee youth soccer team and the transformation of a small American town.

Thorpe, Helen. *The Newcomers: Finding Refuge, Friendship, and Hope in an American Classroom*. New York: Scribner, 2017.
A year-long chronicle of the lives of twenty-two immigrant teenagers as they settle into a high school in Denver.

Uwiringiyimana, Sandra, and Abigail Pesta. *How Dare the Sun Rise: Memoirs of a War Child*. Katherine Tegen Books, 2018.
A girl from the Democratic Republic of Congo survives a massacre and remakes her life in America through art and activism.

HOSPITALITY AND COMMUNITY

Cho, Eugene and Izadi Page, Samira, eds. *No Longer Strangers: Transforming Evangelism with Immigrant Communities*. Grand Rapids: Eerdmans, 2021.
Diverse voices offer guidance on welcoming refugees holistically and with cultural sensitivity.

Glanville, Mark R., and Luke Glanville. *Refuge Reimagined: Biblical Kinship in Global Politics*. Downers Grove: IVP Academic, 2021.
Brothers Mark and Luke offer a deeply theological ethic of kinship that is lived out practically in community.

Oden, Amy G., ed. *And You Welcomed Me: A Sourcebook on Hospitality in Early Christianity*. Nashville: Abingdon, 2001.
A collection of early Christian texts regarding hospitality and its practices.

Pohl, Christine D. *Making Room: Recovering Hospitality as a Christian Tradition*. Grand Rapids: Eerdmans, 1999.
The author revisits the heritage and discipline of welcoming strangers throughout church history.

Van Opstal, Sandra Maria. *The Next Worship: Glorifying God in a Diverse World*. Chicago: InterVarsity Press, 2016.
Likening diverse worship to a sumptuous banquet, Van Opstal shows how worship leaders can set the table and welcome worshipers from every tribe and tongue.

Yong, Amos. *Hospitality & the Other: Pentecost, Christian Practices, and the Neighbor*. Maryknoll: Orbis, 2008.
Yong shows that the religious "other" is not a mere object for conversion but a neighbor to whom hospitality must be both extended and received.

STATEMENTS ON REFUGEES

Below are official statements by various groups regarding refugees:

Evangelical Immigration Table, "Evangelical Statement on Principles for Immigration Reform, 2012."

You can affirm this statement at https://evangelicalimmigrationtable.com/sign-the-principles/.

Global Compact on Refugees (GCR), 2018.

"The first intergovernmentally negotiated agreement, prepared under the auspices of the United Nations, to cover all dimensions of international migration in a holistic and comprehensive manner." See the revised US national statement: https://www.state.gov/global-compact-for-safe-orderly-and-regular-migration-gcm/.

Lausanne Committee for World Evangelization, Mini-Consultation on Reaching Refugees. "No. 5 Thailand Report—Christian Witness to Refugees." Lausanne Committee for World Evangelization, 1980.

An occasional paper drafted by the Lausanne Committee for World Evangelization emerging from the Consultation on World Evangelization held in Pattaya, Thailand in June 1980. This paper representing a collective evangelical voice presents the biblical mandate to protect refugees and offers guidelines for responsible Christian action.

"Strangers No Longer: Together on the Journey of Hope." A Pastoral Letter Concerning Migration by Catholic Bishops of Mexico and the United States, 2003.

https://www.usccb.org/issues-and-action/human-life-and-dignity/immigration/strangers-no-longer-together-on-the-journey-of-hope.

United Nations. "New York Declaration for Migrants and Refugee."

Issued September 15, 2016, at the United Nations Summit for Migrants and Refugees, September 19, 2016, in New York, NY. http://refugeesmigrants.un.org/declaration

World Council of Churches. "A Moment to Choose: Risking to Be with Uprooted People," Statement on Uprooted People, 1995. See also, "A Moment to Choose: Risking to Be with Uprooted People, A Resource Book," 1996.

Adopted in 1995, this "Statement on Uprooted People" addresses uprooted people as a major global crisis.

CARING FOR REFUGEES

Corbett, Steven, and Brian Fikkert. *When Helping Hurts: How to Alleviate Poverty Without Hurting the Poor … and Yourself.* Chicago: Moody Publishers, 2014.

This book shows how some alleviation efforts, failing to consider the complexities of poverty, have actually (albeit unintentionally) done more harm than good.

Kirk, Jeffrey. *10 million to 1: Refugee Resettlement-A How-to Guide.* Bloomington: Balboa Press, 2011.

This book is helpful for those seeking to establish grassroots resettlement teams.

Mollica, Richard F. *Healing Invisible Wounds: Paths to Hope and Recovery in a Violent World.* Nashville: Vanderbilt University Press, 2008.

The director of the Harvard Program in Refugee Trauma celebrates "the capacity of persons to recover from violent events and to engage in self-healing."

EDUCATING CHILDREN ABOUT REFUGEES

Naidoo, Beverly. *Making It Home: Real-Life Stories from Children Forced to Flee.* New York: Dial Books, 2004.

A children's book of testimonies by child refugees. Includes a brief historical introduction to each of the regions of origin of the refugees.

Tavangar, Homa Sabet. *Growing Up Global: Raising Children to Be at Home in the World.* New York: Ballantine Books, 2009.

A hands-on parenting book to help children develop global sensibilities. Filled with creative and practical tips, this book could equally help adults become better global citizens.

We Are Teachers, https://www.weareteachers.com/kids-books-about-refugees/.

This is one example of a book list.

DOCUMENTARIES

Asylum (2003) 20 min, Sandy McLeod and Gini Reticker

> Upon her father insisting that she undergo a circumcision and marry an old man, a young woman escapes Ghana for the United States. Arriving in the US with a phony passport, she was imprisoned by the INS for one year while her asylum case was tried.

Cries from Syria (2017) 1 hr 51 min, Evgeny Afineevsky

> A raw account drawing on hundreds of hours of war footage from the Syrian civil war. Rated MA.

The Donut King (2020) 1 hr 34 min, Alice Gu

> The honest story of a Cambodian refugee who went from rags to riches through his donut store empire, followed by his financial downfall.

God Grew Tired of Us (2006) 89 min, Christopher Dillon Quinn & Tommy Walker

> Orphaned by civil war, the "Lost Boys" of Sudan are granted asylum in the US but struggle to transition to American life.

The Good Lie (2014) 1 hr 50 min, Philippe Falardeu

> Starring Reese Witherspoon, this film captures the story of Sudanese men settling in the Midwest with humor and authenticity.

Human Flow (2017) 2 hr 20 min, Ai Weiwei

> Directed by internationally renowned artist Ai Weiwei, *Human Flow* is a powerful visual expression to forced migration, captured across twenty-three countries.

The Journey to Europe (2016) six-part series, Matthew Cassel

> https://www.matthewcassel.com/the-journey. One Syrian refugee's story to get to Europe and be reunited with his family, who eventually joins him there.

The Letter (2003) 76 min, Ziad H. Hamzeh

> In the wake of 9/11, a firestorm erupts when the mayor of Lewiston, Maine sends a letter to 1,100 newly arrived Somali refugees advising that the city's resources are strained to the limit and requesting that other Somalis not move to the city. Interpreted as racism by some and a rallying cry by white supremacist groups across the US, *The Letter* documents the crossfire of emotions and events.

Lost Boys of Sudan (2004) 87 min, Megan Mylan and Jon Shenk

> An Emmy-nominated feature-length documentary that follows two Sudanese refugees from Sudan and Kenya to the US. Winner of an Independent Spirit Award and two Emmy nominations.

North Korea – Shadows and Whispers (2000) 52 min, Kim Jung-Eun

This documentary, filmed in the remote northeast mountains of China, captures the dire circumstances of North Korean refugees who journey to China.

Overlooked (2020) 11 min, Oliver J. Hughes

This short film asks the question, "Are immigrants a burden or a blessing?" A story about transformation in Kansas City; includes interviews with Jarrett Meek, pastor and executive director of Mission Adelante, a Christian community development center.

Roosevelt's America (2004) 30 min, Roger Weisberg and Tod Lending

The inspirational story of a Liberian refugee who resettles in Chicago and his attempts to reunite with his wife and young daughter, who are still in Liberia. Winner of numerous awards at the Columbus International Film and Video Festival, the San Francisco Black Film Festival, the Cleveland Film Festival, and other venues.

Salam Neighbor (2016) 75 min., Zach Ingrasci and Chris Temple

Two Americans spent one month living inside Za'atari refugee camp among thousands of Syrian refugees. http://livingonone.org/salamneighbor/.

The Split Horn: Life of a Hmong Shaman in America (2001) 60 min, Taggart Siegel

The emotional saga of a Hmong shaman and his family who were transplanted from the mountains of Laos during the Vietnam War to America's heartland. This intimate family portrait explores universal issues of cultural transformation, spirituality and family. For more information: www.pbs.org/splithorn.

Stateless (2020) 1 season, 6 episodes on Netflix

Emma Freeman and Jocelyn Moorhouse
Four lives are intertwined in an Australian immigration detention center.

The Stranger (2014) 40 min, Linda Midgett

Commissioned by the Evangelical Immigration Table, this film profiles three immigrant stories and includes interviews with Christian leaders.

The Trials of Jacob Mach (2013) 23 min, New York Times Documentary

A documentary follows a Lost Boy who, twelve years after leaving Sudan, has found that the dream of a better life is both all around and just outside his grasp.

LISTS OF DOCUMENTARIES AND FILMS

- Refugee Week: https://refugeeweek.org.uk/resources/artists-and-films/online-films/

- Point of View: Do a search on "Immigration" in the Film Archive to pull up over 50 short films and feature films, https://www.pbs.org/pov/film-archive/

- UNHCR: https://www.unhcr.org/innovation/7-videos-guaranteed-to-change-the-way-you-see-refugees/

REFUGEE ASSISTANCE AND MOBILIZATION ORGANIZATIONS AND TOOLS

Boat People SOS (bpsos.org/)

Our goal is to transform victims into survivors and active citizens who reach out and help others like them achieve liberty and dignity.

Christian Community Development Association (ccda.org)

Many of its member organizations serve immigrants and refugees. See website for a directory.

Evangelical Immigration Table (evangelicalimmigrationtable.com/)

Where evangelical Christians of various backgrounds come together to think and act biblically around immigration issues. EIT produces discipleship material, like the "I Was a Stranger" challenge: http://evangelicalimmigrationtable.com/iwasastranger/.

Every Shelter (everyshelter.org)

Building localized refugee-aid ecosystems centered around refugees, including housing solutions, especially in refugee camps

Houston Welcomes Refugees (HWR) (www.houstonwelcomesrefugees.com)

HWR helps ease the resettlement process for newly arrived refugees to Houston by mobilizing volunteers to serve on welcome teams, set up apartments, or donate household items. Disclosure: the author worked for HWR as a program manager for three years.

International Organization for Migration (www.iom.int)

The leading international organization on migration, the IOM is the UN's migration agency, committed to the principle that humane and orderly migration benefits migrants and society.

Office of Refugee Resettlement (US Department of Health and Human Services) (acf.hhs.gov/programs/orr)

Founded on the belief that newly arriving populations have inherent capabilities when given opportunities, the ORR provides people in need with critical resources to assist them in becoming integrated members of American society.

Refugee Council USA (rcusa.org)

A coalition of 22 US-based non-governmental organizations, dedicated to refugee protection, welcome, and excellence in the US refugee resettlement program.

Refugee Highway Partnership (www.refugeehighway.net/)

A collaborative to connect and equip Christians for effective ministry with forcibly displaced people

Refugee Processing Center (www.wrapsnet.org)

The Refugee Processing Center is the creator of WRAPS, a customized computer software system to assist the processing of refugees bound for resettlement in the United States. This website provides State Department reports on refugee arrivals.

Tarjimly (www.tarjim.ly)

This mobile app allows refugees to connect with live translators.

Thrive International (Thriveint.org)

Thrive International specializes in empowering immigrants and citizens through education, affordable housing, and employment programs.

The United Nations High Commission for Refugees (UNHCR) (www.unhcr.org)

This UN agency is mandated to lead and coordinate international action to protect refugees and resolve refugee problems worldwide. The USA for UNHCR link is www.unrefugees.org.

USA Hello (find.usahello.org/#/welcome)

This website/app is translated into multiple languages and helps refugees locate services in their area.

Welcome.US (Welcome.us)

This national initiative formed in 2021 to support Afghan evacuees to the US. Welcome.US is the largest national coalition in resettlement history, with former US presidents and first ladies as honorary co-chairs.

Women of Welcome (womenofwelcome.com)

A community dedicated to understanding God's heart for the immigrant and refugee.

Appendix C

INCREASING YOUR CULTURAL INTELLIGENCE (CQ)

In today's globalized world it's hard to get by without understanding diverse cultures and communication styles. Caring for refugees requires cultural sensitivity and intelligence. Below are a few ideas to help you and your family raise your Cultural Intelligence (CQ).

- **Know the countries of the world.**
  There are over 230 countries on the globe—how many can you identify correctly on a map? Grab an atlas to review and then test yourself using outline maps you can find online.

- **Watch international movies and listen to international music.**
  Get a taste of foreign pop culture. Find out who are the big stars in other countries.

- **Read international memoirs.**
  Memoirs give insight and a personal touch to historical events, what otherwise might be just impersonal facts.

- **Learn a new language.**
  Not only will you gain a useful skill that will help you communicate with newly arrived immigrants, but you will also experience the frustrations that come along with learning a new language, thus helping you empathize with first-time English learners.

- **Try new foods.**
  Visit an ethnic grocery store or a restaurant in an ethnic neighborhood. Broaden your palate, since hospitality and meal-sharing are such a vital part of building friendships.

RECOMMENDED RESOURCES
FOR INCREASING YOUR CULTURAL INTELLIGENCE

Cultural Intelligence Center (culturalq.com) develops four capabilities to boost your cultural intelligence.

Gerzon, Mark. *American Citizen, Global Citizen.* Boulder: Spirit Scope Publishing, 2010.

KnowledgeWorkx (knowledgeworkx.com) provides intercultural intelligence training and consulting to develop individual and organizational cultural agility.

Livermore, David. *Cultural Intelligence: Improving Your CQ to Engage Our Multicultural World.* Grand Rapids: Baker Academic, 2009.

Martin, Jamie C. *Give Your Child the World: Raising Globally Minded Kids One Book at a Time.* Grand Rapids: Zondervan, 2016.

Tavangar, Homa Sabet. *Growing Up Global: Raising Children to Be at Home in the World.* New York: Ballantine Books, 2009.

Appendix D

THE REFUGEE EXPERIENCE

REFUGEE SIMULATION

Several organizations have created simulations or games to give you a glimpse into what refugees have to face. Here are a handful that vary in complexity and length:

- Office of the High Commissioner for Refugees (UNHCR): http://www.unhcr.org/473dc1772.pdf.

- Jesuit Refugee Services: Go to www.jrsusa.org and type in "Walk a Mile in My Shoes" in the search bar.

- Lutheran Immigration and Refugee Services (LIRS): www.lirs.org/refugee-simulation-game.

- Evangelical Covenant Church, The Refugee Journey: covchurch.org/refugeejourney.

WORLD REFUGEE DAY

In addition to participating in a simulation, you could share the refugee experience with your church or community by commemorating World Refugee Day. Every year around June 20, communities around the world organize events "to highlight the plight of refugees under our care and to advocate on their behalf for the help they need." Check to see if your city is organizing a local World Refugee Day.

The following ideas could help you promote World Refugee Day:

- Share personal stories of refugees

- Watch a documentary

- Invite a refugee to speak to your group

- Raise funds for a refugee advocacy organization

- Gather people in prayer

- Invite restaurants that serve the native cuisine of refugees in your community
- For more information, visit www.unrefugees.org.

RIDE WITH REFUGEES

The mission of Ride with Refugees (RwR) is to raise awareness about refugees, engage the community, and promote mobility. Launched in Houston, TX, in 2022 by the author, RwR brings together refugees, community leaders, and refugee-focused non-profits for an organized bike ride and activity fair. Visit www.ridewithrefugees.org for more information.

Appendix E

THE HOSPITALITY OF ABRAHAM'S CHILDREN

In Genesis 18:1–15, we find Abraham, who is sojourning in Hebron (Gen 13:18), sitting by the door of his tent when three visitors pass by. Calling the first one "My Lord," Abraham eagerly offers them food and refreshment. The visitors then remind Abraham and Sarah of the covenant God made to multiply Abraham's future offspring. Various interpretations exist as to the mysterious nature of this visitation. Perhaps the three figures are an early revelation of the Holy Trinity. There is no doubt, however, that hospitality plays a vital role in this interaction, wherein Abraham and Sarah are both tested in their faith.

This episode inspired one of the most famous icons of all time, known as both "The Trinity" and "The Hospitality of Abraham," painted by fifteenth-century Russian artist Andrei Rublev.

The icon and the story behind it also inspired the cover art for this second edition, created by my son, Josiah Wu, age 15, titled "The Hospitality of Abraham's Children." As much as I loved the original cover, I knew I wanted to update the cover art; whereas the first edition of the book focused heavily on data, I wanted this edition to highlight the spiritual elements of refugee welcome, especially hospitality, hence the decision to ask Josiah to emulate the Rublev icon, as many other artists have done (try an internet search to see).

The four figures represent unique individuals from around the world, diverse in age, gender, religion, and nationality. They all sit on a richly woven welcome mat, similar to the meals my family has shared in Afghan homes. The addition of a fourth, smaller figure symbolizes the magnitude of the current refugee crisis; it also represents the fact that half of all refugees are children. The textured golden background creates a timeless look and hearkens to the ancient Christian practice of hospitality toward strangers. And the tree is a creation symbol, reminding us that all God's people are made in his image. The vision of this book is that the "hospitality of Abraham's children" will bring forth scenarios in which diverse people are seated together at the table (or welcome mat) of fellowship, the fruit of faithfulness to God's commands to welcome the strangers in our midst.

> *If we are to love our neighbors, before doing anything*
> *else we must see our neighbors. With our imagination*
> *as well as our eyes, that is to say like artists, we must see*
> *not just their faces but the life behind and within their*
> *faces. Here it is love that is the frame we see them in.*
> *–Frederick Buechner*

BIBLIOGRAPHY

Bohmer, Carol and Amy Shuman. *Rejecting Refugees: Political Asylum in the 21st Century.* London: Routledge, 2008.

Bonomolo, Alessandro, and Stephanie Kirchgaessner. "U.N. Says 800 Migrants Dead in Boat Disaster as Italy Launches Rescue of Two More Vessels." *The Guardian*, April 20, 2015, https://www.theguardian.com/world/2015/apr/20/italy-pm-matteo-renzi-migrant-shipwreck-crisis-srebrenica-massacre.

Buttrick, George Arthur, ed. *The Interpreter's Dictionary of the Bible*, Volume 4. Nashville: Abingdon Press, 1962.

Cambodian Mutual Assistance Association of Greater Lowell, Inc., http://www.cmaalowell.org/wp/.

Chacour, Elias, with David Hazard. *Blood Brothers: The Dramatic Story of a Palestinian Christian Working for Peace in Israel.* Grand Rapids: Chosen Books, 2003.

Chandler, Diana. "To Love, Not Fear Refugees Focus of GC2 Summit." *Baptist Press*, January 21, 2016, https://www.baptistpress.com/resource-library/news/to-love-not-fear-refugees-focus-of-gc2-summit/.

Davenport, Carol, and Campbell Robertson. "Resettling the First 'Climate Refugees.'" *New York Times*, May 3, 2016. http://www.nytimes.com/2016/05/03/us/resettling-the-first-american-climate-refugees.html.

De Pillis, Lydia, Kulwant Saluja, and Denise Lu. "A Visual Guide to 75 Years of Major Refugee Crises around the World." *Washington Post.* https://www.washingtonpost.com/graphics/world/historical-migrant-crisis/.

Donahue, Patrick, and Arne Delfs. "Germany Saw 1.1 Million Migrants in 2015 as Debate Intensifies." *Bloomberg*, January 6, 2016, https://www.bloomberg.com/news/articles/2016-01-06/germany-says-about-1-1-million-asylum-seekers-arrived-in-2015.

Donico, Mary Yu, ed. "Cambodian Americans." In *Asian American Society: An Encyclopedia.* Thousand Oaks: SAGE, 2014.

Engel, Pamela. "Trump on Syrian Refugees: 'Lock Your Doors, Folks.'" *Business Insider*, April 25, 2016. http://www.businessinsider.com/trump-syrian-refugees-isis-2016-4.

Forché, Carolyn. "The Boatman." *Poetry*, October 2016.

GC2 Summit. http://www.gc2summit.com/statement/.

GC2 Summit Statement. "Christian Declaration on Caring for Refugees: An Evangelical Response." http://www.reconciliationjusticenetwork.com/wp-content/uploads/2016/02/GC2-Summit-Declaration.pdf.

Gjelten, Tom, and Marisa Peñaloza. "Built by Immigrants, US Catholic Churches Bolstered by Them Once Again." National Public Radio, September 9, 2015, http://www.npr.org/2015/09/09/437219447/built-by-immigrants-u-s-catholic-churches-bolstered-by-them-once-again.

Internal Displacement Monitoring Centre. www.internal-displacement.org.

Johnson, Todd M. "USA Evangelicals/Evangelicals in a Global Context." *Lausanne World Pulse*, January 2006.

Johnson, Todd M., and Cindy M. Wu. *Our Global Families: Christians Embracing Common Identity in a Changing World*. Grand Rapids: Baker Academic, 2009.

Kingsley, Patrick. "More than 700 Migrants Feared Dead in Mediterranean Sinkings." *The Guardian*, May 29, 2016, https://www.theguardian.com/world/2016/may/29/700-migrants-feared-dead-mediterranean-says-un-refugees.

Lang, Jia Lynn. *One Mighty and Irresistible Tide: The Epic Struggle Over American Immigration, 1924–1965*. New York: W. W. Norton, 2021.

Migration Policy Institute. "US Annual Refugee Resettlement Ceilings and Number of Refugees Admitted, 1980-Present." https://www.migrationpolicy.org/programs/data-hub/charts/us-refugee-resettlement.

Missing Migrants Project. https://missingmigrants.iom.int/mediterranean.

Mylan, Megan, and Jon Shenk. "Lost Boys of Sudan." 2004. http://www.lostboysfilm.com/.

Naidoo, Beverly. *Making It Home: Real-Life Stories from Children Forced to Flee*. New York: Dial Books, 2004.

National Archives Foundation. "Refugee Act of 1980." https://www.archivesfoundation.org/documents/refugee-act-1980/.

Nouwen, Henri J. M. *With Open Hands*. Notre Dame: Ave Maria Press, 1972.

Office of the United Nations High Commissioner for Refugees. *The State of the World's Refugees: Human Displacement in the New Millenium*. Oxford: Oxford University Press, 2006.

Pipher, Mary. *The Middle of Everywhere: The World's Refugees Come to Our Town*. New York: Harcourt, 2002.

Pohl, Christine. *Making Room: Recovering Hospitality as a Christian Tradition*. Grand Rapids: Eerdmans, 1999.

Refugee Processing Center. www.wrapsnet.org.

Sacks, Jonathan. "Loving the Stranger." February 8, 2008, http://www.rabbisacks.org/covenant-conversation-5768-mishpatim-loving-the-stranger/.

Soerens, Matthew, and Jenny Hwang. *Welcoming the Stranger: Justice, Compassion and Truth in the Immigration Debate*. Downers Grove: InterVarsity Press, 2009.

United Nations High Commissioner for Refugees. "More than 100 Million Are Forcibly Displaced." https://www.unhcr.org/refugee-statistics/insights/explainers/100-million-forcibly-displaced.html.

United Nations High Commissioner for Refugees Resettlement Handbook 2011. www.unhcr.org/46f7c0ee2.pdf.

United Nations High Commissioner for Refugees. "Solutions." http://www.unhcr.org/en-us/solutions.html.

University of Massachusetts Boston Institute for Asian American Studies. "Population of Asian Americans in Selected Cities and Towns in Massachusetts." https://www.umb.edu/iaas/census/2010/population_of_asian_americans_cities_towns_in_ma.

US Citizenship and Immigration Services. "Immigration and Naturalization Service Refugee Law and Policy Timeline, 1891–2003." https://www.uscis.gov/about-us/our-history/history-office-and-library/featured-stories-from-the-uscis-history-office-and-library/refugee-timeline.

US Citizenship and Immigration Services. "Refugee Processing and Security Screening." https://www.uscis.gov/humanitarian/refugees-and-asylum/refugees/refugee-processing-and-security-screening.

US Department of State, Bureau of Population, Refugees, and Migration. "Summary of Refugee Admissions, 2016."

Vine, W. E. *Vines's Complete Expository Dictionary of Old and New Testament Words*. Nashville: Thomas Nelson, 1996.

Visit us at missionbooks.org

Refugee Diaspora:
Missions amid the Greatest Humanitarian Crisis of the World

Miriam Adeney and Sam George, Editors

These hope-filled pages of refugees encountering Jesus presents models of Christian ministry from the front lines of the refugee crisis and the real challenges of ministering to today's refugees. It includes biblical, theological, and practical reflections on mission in diverse diaspora contexts from leading scholars as well as practitioners in all major regions of the world.

Paperback & ePub

A Hybrid World:
Diaspora, Hybridity, and Missio Dei

Sadiri Joy Tira and Juliet Lee Uytanlet, Editors

This book is the product of a global consultation of church and mission leaders who discussed the implications of hybridity in the mission of God. The contributors draw from their collective experiences and perspectives, explore emerging concepts and initiatives, and ground them in authoritative Scripture for application to the challenges that hybridity presents to global missions.

Paperback & ePub

WILLIAM CAREY PUBLISHING

CPSIA information can be obtained
at www.ICGtesting.com
Printed in the USA
BVHW010016131022
649106BV00005B/7

9 781645 084525